Kebrina Josefina DeJean

Awakening
THROUGH
MOMENTS *of* CHOICE
A MEMOIR OF DIVINE GUIDANCE

MEANING • connection • Love • Truth
1) shred limit belief
2) open possibilities
3) Living op purpose + personal desires -
I am a creative Being, Born to express the Power of the cosmos through manifestation of my daily life.

VINCE KRAMER & MARY KRAMER
FOREWORD BY KAREN CURRY PARKER

Cover design by Kristina Edstrom

An Imprint for GracePoint Publishing (www.GracePointPublishing.com)

GracePoint Matrix, LLC
624 S. Cascade Ave, Suite 201
Colorado Springs, CO 80903
www.GracePointMatrix.com
Email: Admin@GracePointMatrix.com
SAN # 991-6032

A Library of Congress Control Number has been requested and is pending.

ISBN: (Paperback) 978-1-955272-45-2
eISBN: 978-1-955272-46-9
.

Books may be purchased for educational, business, or sales promotional use.
For bulk order requests and price schedule contact:
Orders@GracePointPublishing.com

To our family and friends that have supported us in our awakenings and in sharing this book with the world.

Contents

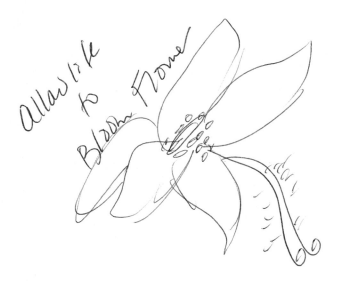

Source

Certainty — cosmic — clarity

Connection

unity
internal
motivation

Accelerate &
proActive

Full
|| courage of an open heart

|| open spiritual 👁👁
quantum leap of faith —

virtuous will
Foreword
True embodiment of
self purpose

interesting?

Foreword

The mystical path is not for cowards.

To truly step out as spiritual teachers and leaders like Vince and Mary have done, you have to be willing eschew the trappings of the human condition and boldly emerge as your true self.

In other words, you have to stop being "normal".

What exactly is "normal"? For many of us, "normal" means we shut down our innate connection to Source, to all the cosmic helpers who work through us to help us fully manifest the purpose, and the potential of our lives.

"Normal" means we close our spiritual eyes and buy into the lies that caused us to internalize the message that it's not okay for us to be who we truly are and how we truly are. "Normal" means we deny our hearts, our inner knowing of what we sense is Truth, we cut ourselves off from our joy and the infinite lineage of who we truly are.

To a certain degree, we've learned to close our eyes and be "normal" because it's easier—at least in the short run. When we're normal we don't have to take quantum leaps of faith. We don't have to contend with doubt. We plod along in our daily lives fulfilling what we know we can, by virtue of our work and our will.

But, we can only push so far with our will. At a time when the planet is facing challenges that require great leaps of faith and the skill of knowing how to consciously choose different options for humanity, we need people who are awake, connected, conscious, and aware.

In this beautiful book, Vince shares the story of his transformation from a "normal" middle-class man with a "normal" job as a pilot into an aligned, awakened, conscious channel who shares information with people to help them connect more deeply with their purpose in this lifetime. You're going to read about how Vince boldly embraced his true purpose, choice by choice by choice.

The work of living on purpose requires not only the courage to show up with your Heart exposed to the world, but it also requires the courage to turn inward, to be willing to explore your inner landscape and to be honest about what caused you to stop being the magical cosmic being you are in the first place.

You have to be willing to let go of old stories that limit you, release doubt and untangle yourself for ancestral narratives that have kept you trapped in patterns of self-sabotage and denial for your entire life. You have to be vulnerable and honest. You have to be willing to reconstruct your life and release that which no longer serves you. You have to let go and trust in things that are often unseen. You have to grapple with the unknown.

As Vince shares with us, each twist and turn of this inner journey brings choices. Vince didn't just wake up one day and begin to channel. His journey was incremental. As each layer of remembering dropped in, Vince proceeded on the journey of embodying his purpose. Through the story of his journey, he invites us to courageously proceed on our own journey of remembering, step-by-step, choice-by-choice.

Equipped with the knowledge and experience from his own journey, Vince has cultivated gifts that he now uses to accelerate the journey of awakening with others. Even though his personal story of awakening happened over years, what he learned and the wisdom that he shares gives you the insights you need to embody your true purpose with ease, support and courage.

Vince's story paves the way for others and reveals what is possible when we surrender to the truth of who we are. As Vince assures us in this book, joy awaits us when we remember our Divine nature.

Now more than ever, we need people like Vince and Mary who so courageously remind us that we are more than just humans living an Earth story. We are creative beings, born to express the power of the cosmos through the manifestations of our daily lives.

The more we embody the truth of who we are, the easier it will be to discover the elegant solutions to the challenges facing humanity today.

The single most important thing we need to do on the planet at this time is to wake up to who we are and to live true to the purpose we co-created with Source when we chose to emerge on the planet during this powerful time of transition. We are being called to remember that we are all one, that our individual lives deeply impact the lives of others and that our joy and alignment creates an evolving world of peace.

Karen Curry Parker
September 2022

Prologue
Mary Shares Her Story

This book and the stories in it are about Vince's awakening, his learning to accept guidance, and his willingness to take action. His growth and expansion have allowed him to fully live his purpose. Together we founded Imagine Miracles to help others do the same. It is a transformational and personal growth company designed and dedicated to help people find their true selves and live the life they are meant to live.

We all need and attract others to help trigger our awakenings and walk with us as we learn and expand into our purpose. I provided it for Vince on his journey. My awakening was the precursor to the adventure you are about to read. It wasn't an awakening. In many ways, I never really forgot; I remembered mentally so I couldn't forget, but I did nothing with it. My awakening would happen many years later when Vince's awakening helped to open the door for mine. That is when I started to live my purpose.

I started my life in Northern California in the 1960s only fifteen miles from Berkeley. At the time, my sisters—ten and eleven years older—were approaching their teens and looked and acted like typical sixties-era teenagers. My oldest sister Norah was very much a hippie, a free spirit. I didn't understand then that the hippie way of life was an expansion of consciousness—from the old paradigm of materialism, competition, and externally motivated happiness to a new paradigm of unity, inward focus, and internal motivation. Norah, always attuned to this awareness, influenced my mother in ways I would grow to understand later.

My mom sought knowledge and self-improvement through workshops and education as we grew up. She had many mentors that shaped her life and influenced mine. This cultivated an environment of freedom to keep the intuitive connection we are all born with and most of us lose. I never lost the connection, but it was never cultivated either. I knew I had a strong intuition, and in fact, I trusted it over anyone's advice in my life and anything I learned in school. There were two phenomena that happened to me which never let me forget I was more than just my mind and my body.

The first happened when I was about twelve years old while visiting my sister Bev and her husband John. Around two in the morning, a white orb of light appeared as if it came down and out of the fireplace. I was almost asleep on the sofa in the living room when I opened my eyes to see this orb float out of the hearth and bob and weave around the room and me. I sat up initially terrified and spellbound, but I also had a warm reassuring feeling in the center of my chest as I continued to watch it for what seemed like a half hour before it just disappeared. I knew somehow it was important and I couldn't wait to ask Bev about it in the morning. Bev, the most grounded of my sisters, listened intently and gently reassured me she had no idea what it was and to forget about it. As much as I worshiped my big sister and wanted to do what she thought was best for me, I just couldn't.

The second phenomena happened almost three years later. I was fifteen and hanging out with a friend who had a lot of experience in metaphysical teachings. He was the nephew of Dr. Brugh Joy, a mentor of my mom's. Dr. Joy was a distinguished and respected member of the Los Angeles medical community. He contracted a life-threatening disease that left him very weak and sometimes delirious. One of those delusional episodes culminated in an illuminating meditation, which caused him to abruptly give up his medical practice. Six weeks after his meditation, he discovered that his illness was totally cured. This experience pushed him to further his explorations into realms of healing involving energy, the chakra system, meditation, and higher levels of consciousness. He was a major influence for my mother, his children, and me.

Dr. Joy's nephew, Daven and I were sitting cross legged on the floor of the fully furnished guest cottage in the back of his parents' home. The wood within the room emitted a fresh, woodsy smell, and the floor-to-ceiling windows let in warm sunshine on a cool, coastal day.

"Do you want to see something really cool?" he asked. I nodded. He continued, "Hold out your hands in front of you and close your eyes."

I extended my arms fully with my hands out straight, my fingers together and my palms facing him. He did the same with his palms facing me, but he left a space of about twelve inches between our hands. Suddenly, I felt the warmth of his hands even though he wasn't touching me.

He continued his instructions, "Slowly move your hands away from mine, then slowly move them towards mine again. Do you feel the resistance?"

I was spellbound by the warmth and pressure that was building between our hands. With my eyes still closed I whispered, "Yes!"

Daven said, "That is the energy building. Now, gently open your eyes and focus on the energy you can feel building between our hands."

As I fluttered my eyes open, I could only see his hands and mine. I had such focus. I looked to see if his eyes were open too. He looked directly at me then back to our hands.

"Follow my hands as we make a ball with the energy," he said as he began to cup his hands.

It was like we were creating a ball of clay together but without our hands touching. The connection was intense. I had never felt such peace and excitement at the same time. I didn't want this experience to end. All of a sudden there was a white ball or orb of light bobbing up and down between our hands just like the one I saw floating in my sister's living room. As I looked at Daven, I saw he was experiencing pure joy. Clearly, he had done this before and was confident that we could do it. I was amazed.

Then with his mission accomplished, he said with the gentlest voice, "Yes, we did it!" And just like that the ball of white light disappeared.

We repeated these light experiences many times after that. Each one was even more powerful and exciting. I had to have answers. I had to know how and why. Those answers would not come for another thirteen years.

Three years later, while working and commuting, I had another spiritual experience. I was set up for a date by a friend who thought we would be a great match. I felt calm, with a little anxiety and anticipation. I never would have imagined meeting my future husband could be spiritual, but it was.

I was set up by a mutual friend to meet Russ at his house. When I arrived, I grabbed the gold doorknob, turned it, and opened it to a handsome man with a huge smile on his face. I looked into his eyes and returned the smile instantly.

After what felt like five minutes, I said, "Hi!"

He continued smiling and said, "Shall we go get a coffee?"

"Yes, of course," I said.

He didn't act like anything was strange, but I was taken aback by what had happened; it was as if time had stopped. I asked myself as

genuine & vulnerability

we walked down the stairs and along the sidewalk to his car, *Is this a sign?* I took it as one.

As I'm known to do, I stepped fully into this relationship without looking back. By the time several months had passed however, I was too entrenched in the promise of this alliance to heed a warning sign. We were driving across the Bay Bridge heading toward his home in San Francisco having a conversation about my previous spiritual experiences. He looked at me and simply stated, "I don't believe in this stuff, and I won't have anything to do with it." I looked him in the eyes until he turned quickly away. *Was it to keep his eyes on the road or to avoid me?* It didn't feel right.

I ignored the intuitive hit in my body which felt like a tightening of my heart area, and I plunged ahead saying, "Ok, no problem."

It was at that very moment I decided I just wouldn't talk to him about it anymore, so I shut my heart down and I moved fully into my head, committing to living an average, logical life. We were married within months, destined to be like everyone else.

Six and a half years later, my mom disrupted everything.

The TV was on in the background with news about the Gulf War as the phone rang. "Hi Mom," I said. "How are you?"

She succinctly reported how she was doing and then said, "Mary, I need to send you some information. I've got a lot to tell you. But I want you to listen to a recording and then we'll talk."

"What kind of recording?" I asked

"It's a channeling of St. Germain, and he's teaching the world about twin flame unions."

I replied, "Channeling?"

She answered, "Yes, I've found a woman who literally is the physical voice of what's called an Ascended Master, one who is in spirit form, but is meant to teach the world some pretty amazing and life-altering lessons. Stuff that I've shared with you over the years is really driven home by the sheer genius that comes through this person. But the part I really want you to sit with is about twin flame unions. I feel like there's something there for you. I can't explain it, but I hope you'll be open to it. What do you think?"

Intrigued, I replied, "Okay, that sounds interesting."

We said our goodbyes, and I put my attention back on the news of the war. I knew in the pit of my stomach my comfortable life was going to be disrupted by this recording and what my mom had to say.

Indeed, listening to this first recording caused a deep disruption inside of me.

My heart was being awakened by the energy of the words. In fact, it would open more and more with all the recordings my mom would later send. I learned new concepts that contradicted all the ways of thinking I had adopted. Ways of being a good citizen, being right no matter how it might affect the other person, and the endless pursuit of the "perfect life" were just a few. All of these beliefs rooted in the paradigm of materialism and competition were being rattled and shaken as I learned about oneness, community, energy, and connection. By that time, I was intrigued and had to meet St. Germain in person—through a channel that is.

One very cold day in February of 1992, our sons Lloyd and Riley were with us in our 4Runner, safely buckled in their car seats. It was about six weeks after my youngest, Riley, was born. Russ, the boys, and I were barreling across Interstate 70 to spend a week in San Jose, California with his mother, Mimi with whom I had a very close relationship—I was the daughter she never had. She was in her seventies, and I was only twenty-eight.

For most of the twenty-hour drive, I was either taking care of the kids or lost in thought—*How can I pull off spending an entire day away from family, leaving my six-week-old baby? Will I be able to accomplish the trip without telling the whole truth? I know the day in Tiburon is going to change my life, but I don't know how.*

Driving alone up Highway 101 to Tiburon, I was full of excitement for what lay ahead with my mom, yet full of guilt for lying and having left my two babies for the day. I told Russ and Mimi I was going shopping with my mom in the city, a believable and favorite pastime of ours.

I parked the car on a hilly street in Tiburon being careful to turn the wheels away from the curb. The sky was brilliant blue, and I felt the sun on my face as I made my way from the car to the front door of the house where my mom was living with her friends. I hardly knew anything about her friends, just that they were bringing the teachings of St. Germain, an Ascended Master, by giving seminars and small talks. The channel's name was Angel. I rang the bell and was warmly welcomed by Sterling, Angel's husband. He was very tall and had to stoop a bit to give me a hug. I looked past him to see my mom and Angel sitting at the breakfast table in the sunny nook at the end of a long hall. As I approached them, they asked about my drive up and did everything to make sure I was comfortable. I shared that I was so excited for our day together, but I had to make the drive to San Jose and be back to Mimi's by dark.

I enjoyed catching up with my mom and getting to know the interesting couple. Finally, the time came, and I walked upstairs with the three of them. We went to a room dedicated to Angel's channelings. Angel was a very small woman with blonde hair. She looked tiny in the straight-back chair, and I sat down across from her. She smiled warmly at me and closed her eyes. I didn't know what to expect, but I was ready for anything. After only a few minutes, her lids opened and looking back at me were the most penetrating energetic eyes I had ever seen. I held my breath.

She opened her mouth and said in a voice that wasn't her own, "Good afternoon. We have waited a long time to speak with you, and what an aligned time it is for what will come to open your heart

I attract my partner
I attract clarity
I attract health, wealth, happiness

and mind to the possibilities beyond what you can imagine in the now. There are things beyond what you believe is possible if you but open your heart and mind. No one on Earth is any more special than the other, yet each is so special and unique that all must show up fully and step into who they are." I was mesmerized.

The voice continued, "I am St. Germain, and I come today to assist you and plant a seed for you to move from a place of materialism into the fullness of having everything you want in abundance and being able to experience life in any way that you want without feeling that you need to compete with someone else to have it, or that if you have it, someone else won't, or if they have it, you can't. Abundance comes from the willingness, the understanding, and the ability for each and every one of you to attract everything into your life that you want. You believe that the high vibration, the joy, and the happiness comes from the achievement of the outside, but as you step into the understanding, you will see that it's achieved on the inside. It's a matter of uncovering it from the *inside*. It's finding the abundance in who you are and what you're here to bring to the world that really creates the fun, joy, and excitement of being able to attract those things in your life that are in alignment with you to live in that way."

As the energy overwhelmed me like being on a roller coaster, I heard the voice continue.

Honestly, though I heard the voice, I don't think I was listening anymore. My body felt like I was in fight or flight survival mode with heart racing and muscles tight—the effects of a surge of adrenaline. There was a part of me that was in full protection mode because it knew my life was going to change forever. It knew that I would not be the same person ever again. I could never forget these words. My mind started racing too. I wanted St. Germain to continue to talk to me, yet I realized I had only so much time to get my questions answered.

My life is full of abundance and I attract all that I want for my life. I believe I receive I achieve my own happiness.

My attention was snapped back to the small room and the channel when I heard him say, "What questions do you have for me?"

With my heart pounding and my head racing I asked him, "Why do I remember the orb in Florida? That was over ten years ago!"

Angel smiled—or St. Germain smiled—at me and explained, "It was intended to be an enigma to you. Something to keep your attention on what is unseen."

He was right, I couldn't forget that night with the orb. And then I remembered playing with the energy ball with Daven. "Was that the same thing?" I asked.

"Yes," he replied, "and there were many more energetic experiences that you just don't remember. But that is okay because they served their purpose to keep you connected to your knowingness about energy."

I was satisfied with that answer, and I knew I was running out of time, so I rushed into my next question which was my deepest darkest secret, "Why do I *not* want to be married anymore? I have two children! I've been with this man for ten years. We have a great life. Please help me."

I started to relax as I felt this warm energy emanating from Angel's eyes blanketing me with a sense that everything is in Divine Order and not to worry.

He continued saying, "The soul agreement that you and Russ have was completed with the birth of your second child. You and he are complete."

I was totally in shock, but somehow, I felt incredible excitement deep inside of me. I yearned for more, and I always thought the "more" I yearned for was a better house, a better car, or more vacations. I still wanted those things, but this feeling urged me to ask for other information to help me.

Everything is in Divine order - All is well in my world

"Then who am I supposed to be with and why?" I asked him, desperate to know.

Continuing to feel the warm connection and comfort, I concentrated on him as he explained that I would attract into my life a twin flame. Even though I had heard this term on the recordings my mom sent me, I asked him to explain what a twin flame was.

"The energy of the flame which emanates from God splits, and two souls emerge. The two life streams are corresponding, meaning that they begin the spiritual path together and often share similar interests, therefore, their paths are considered parallel," he explained.

Okay, then I was really excited. "You mean I will attract someone that has the deepest possible connection to me? And I will recognize him?"

"Yes," he replied, "and there is one more thing I want to share with you before you go today."

"Oh please, tell me." I requested.

"There is an energy that wants to come to you in the form of a girl, but you will need the match of a twin flame to bring this energy onto the Earth plane." St. Germain was continuing, but I couldn't take in anymore. He obviously sensed that because he said, "Ok Mary, I believe I have given you enough to think about."

Once again that snapped my attention back to him and I said, "Thank you so much. I can't wait to speak with you again."

He ended our session with, "Until another now, Namaste."

And just like that he was gone.

I heard Angel say, "How was it?"

I don't remember my answer.

The sun was getting lower over the water, and I knew I had to get back to San Jose. I thanked Angel and Sterling profusely, hugged my mom goodbye, and hit the road with the audio tape from my first channeling in hand.

I listened to the recording the first chance I could get which was my turn driving on our way back to Colorado Springs. Russ was resting his eyes from driving. He was sitting in the passenger seat and the boys were quiet in the back. As I took my position as driver, I adjusted my Walkman earphones over my head and pushed play as I put the truck in gear and started driving, listening to every word.

Over the course of the recording, I heard way more than I had remembered from that life-changing session. During the first few days back in the reality of family life, I tried to remember the details, but really, all I could remember was the feeling, the energy. I wanted that energy back. It was the beginning of creating a new reality for me: the pursuit of living a higher vibration.

And it was also the beginning of the end of my marriage.

I tried; boy did I try. I never shared what I was listening to. It was the beginning of many made-up stories. I knew my life was changing trajectory and it felt like I needed to share something so Russ wouldn't be completely blindsided. Hesitantly, I told him where I had gone, and I expressed the importance of the message and the energy in my life. I even added that if he couldn't support me in seeking, I would leave. While he did promise he would be more openminded, he didn't deliver.

I lived a separate spiritual life searching for my twin flame while I lived in a loveless marriage awaiting the signs for the right time. I knew I would never be able to leave on my own volition, but I knew I *would* leave if I could just figure out how.

While I heard the call for something more, I was locked into trying to make something work that simply didn't. I was making myself sick: living a life of separation, seeking spirituality, longing for my twin flame. After fourteen years, my heart literally couldn't take it anymore.

Live Life → Higher vibration
Book → Reading

The doctor opened the door to the examining room, and he had a look of shock on his face as he said, "Hi Mary. What in the hell are you doing here?"

"Hi Ron. Well, I think I have a heart issue."

He pulled his stool over next to me, looked me directly in the eyes and said, "Mary, stress will kill you. This is not a joke. Get into therapy immediately." ♡ ♡ ♡

Instead of being terrified, I felt seen. I felt relieved.

I started therapy, which helped me see my part in why my marriage was such a disaster, but more importantly, I found a channel who reinforced what I knew to be true, but at a higher vibration. I felt called to revisit a local metaphysical fair where I'd been many times in fourteen years. A gifted channel, Eloryia, was offering a retreat at her home, which I immediately signed up for.

Thanks to my new understanding from the therapist and the retreat with Eloryia, things at home went from the status quo to unbridled chaos. I couldn't hold back anymore and this new version of me was met with much resistance. I gave up and just stopped caring about anything. But a funny thing happened along the way, I came alive and started fighting my way back to me.

I had two teenage boys, a flourishing career, and was responsible for a team of people. How was I ever going to get what I wanted by leaving all of that?

I knew I couldn't do it alone; I needed divine guidance, but I didn't know how to ask for that—until I found the book *Divine Prescriptions* by Doreen Virtue. It was a book I hoped would help me find my twin flame.

As I stepped into the hot bath water, I lit the last of the many candles on the edge of the tub. I settled back with my book in hand, and I prayed. Actually, it was more of an incantation than a prayer. I said out loud, "Dear Guardian Angel of my future soulmate, I ask your assistance in helping me to recognize and meet him. Please help me attain the health and happiness I need in order to be a compatible partner to my soulmate. Please arrange for circumstances so that we can find one another. Guide me very clearly with explicit instructions so I will meet my soulmate without delay. Please help me to stay peaceful and serene during the time before I meet my soulmate and help me to stay filled with peace and inner love. Thank you." I put the book down on the tile shelf.

It took two messengers for me to recognize and meet the twin flame I was looking for. Two men that came into my life for short periods of time, both to help me prepare for the life that would come from meeting my twin flame. Of course, the twin flame I was seeking was Vince.

The first messenger showed up within six weeks of my prayer to the guardian angel. This man co-created with me the opportunity to move out of my long marriage.

The second messenger co-created with me the heart opening I needed to recognize Vince. Even though I was in hot pursuit of my twin flame since the channeling in Tiburon, I couldn't even be conscious of meeting Vince five years later because my heart was closed, and I was living my life through my mind. It took another ten years to see him.

He was right there the entire time.

my truth Flame.
Pray For higher self
ancestors
parent
friends
family

A wake-up call brings us to a moment of choice.

Do we choose to step into being the creator of our life or do we allow ourselves to be a victim?

I am the creator & manifestor of my life.

We have free will and although we have this unique purpose, we still can choose to step into it or not. We can choose to find ways to learn and grow and support ourselves through it or we can choose to believe life is happening to us and choose inaction. As we learn and grow and increase our level of awareness, we can choose to stay the same or fully move into who we truly are.

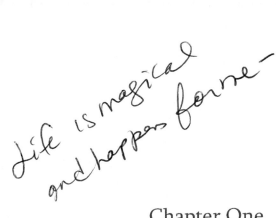

Life is magical and happens for me —

Chapter One
Something is Missing

When you live from the outside in trying to find happiness and fulfillment, there will always be something missing. The happiness and fulfillment come from inside you. Then it can be shared with the outside world.

The Round Table, channeled by Vince Kramer

Just as he got to me, a bulletin with a "Breaking News" banner flashed across the bottom of the TV on the office wall. A third airplane had just hit the Pentagon building in Washington, DC. There was no doubt in my mind, we were under attack, and they were using *our* airplanes as weapons. I felt the anger build in me as I noticed my body getting unusually hot. At the same time, the chaos of the fear of not knowing what I could do to help the hundreds of flight crews still in the air flooded my system.

Were there more bombs flying around the skies of the world? And then it hit me, *Where are my friends?* I knew hundreds of pilots that flew for all the airlines. My thoughts were rapid and overwhelming, and my head was trying to process all of them at once.

The urgency of the last broadcast subsided, and it was time for me to get my marching orders from Ray, the emergency response coordinator. I was the flight operations representative to the Airbus fleet emergency response team. Not knowing if an Airbus was involved, we had to prepare for the worst-case scenario.

I learned my lessons well.

I used everything I learned—the ways of others, including my grandfather and the people I thought had it all—to live my life. Just like I was taught, I competed, never let great be good enough, and never allowed myself to settle for second place.

Many of us learned to tie our success, fulfillment, and happiness to the outside world because of the rules we learned from prior generations. There were examples of what they shared all around us as we were growing up. We looked at what seemed to make others happy and then believed that if it made them happy, it surely would do that for us. Some of us strove for the promotion, raise, or bonus. Others pursued the house, boat, or car believing that would fill the "what is missing" gap. Others tried to keep up with the neighbors because they believed that might fill the void. We have been inundated by media that tells us the magical answer is in the right car, restaurant, cologne, or relationship.

Society measures our success and happiness by the job we hold, the money we make. or the level of education we have. The neighborhood we live in, or the size of our house can also be a measuring stick. Much of my report card was based on competition. Like me, most of us have been taught to compete and win, to always be the best.

It didn't take long for me to stop competing against others and start competing against myself. When the things I did, the jobs I got, and the stuff I acquired didn't bring the happiness and fulfillment I thought they would, I set out to be, do, and have more. It meant that I didn't do enough or that I would need to do more. Surely, I'd find what would make me happy, and I have met many who feel the same way. I have also met many who just settled because they had beliefs that kept them from moving forward.

When we don't measure up or we don't find the happiness we want and deserve. We have the tendency to look to the next thing or person that will make us feel better. We strive for more or bigger. In some cases, we just give up and stop trying. We blame it on our environment or opportunities.

I blamed myself, and pushed myself harder and further, and unfortunately, I pushed myself further away from me.

I blamed it all on myself. It was my fault I couldn't find that magic combination. Just like when I was younger, I kept telling myself that I could have done better. The only difference as an adult was that I was saying the words and not my grandfather. By most standards, I had it all, though it didn't feel that way.

As I sat in the solitude of my backyard, I had the all-too-familiar ache of something missing. I knew there had to be more to life. Just like the songs of the birds in the trees around me, I was experiencing the looping thoughts rhythmically playing in my head.

I'd been in management at United Airlines for eight years. I had steadily moved up in title and responsibility. I enjoyed my job, and I liked making a difference thanks to my position as the Assistant Chief Pilot for one of the airline's biggest fleets. My main responsibilities included training development, compliance, and supervising the evaluator cadre. Basically, I was responsible for the operations and safety of the fleet from the pilot or flight operations' perspective. It was an amazing job and one that I was proud to have;

it gave me a chance to use my talents and gifts. I improved the quality of training and helped many find opportunities for personal growth and promotion.

Yet there was still something missing, and I wasn't completely happy.

I was enjoying the solitude of sitting in nature and the time alone to consider my confusion. In looking for answers, I allowed myself to go back to the last time I felt this way. I easily remembered every detail. It was many years before, but it felt extremely familiar.

I had just returned from the first Gulf War, Desert Storm. I was home a few weeks and received orders to attend a professional military course in Alabama. I enjoyed the course thoroughly and was recognized as a distinguished graduate. I loved military life.

Throughout my military career, I was able to learn and grow in ways that afforded me promotions and positions beyond my rank. I enjoyed the challenges and the work. I was constantly competing against myself. I wanted to make a difference, I wanted to excel, and I wanted to move into positions where I could do more. Graduating with distinction from this school would help in my qualifications to do just that. My time in Desert Storm and 105 combat flying hours in my logbook didn't hurt my chances either in living my plan.

Similar to the feelings from eighteen years earlier in the military, I felt something was missing from my life at United. I recognized the pattern as I remembered.

I was one of two of my Air Force unit's standardization and evaluator pilots at the time. Everyone had left the office hours before, and I had just finished up the day's paperwork. I noticed an unopened envelope on the corner of my desk next to the model of the EC-135 that I have learned to love. I'm not sure why I hadn't noticed it earlier.

"Captain Vincent Kramer." Yep, it's for me.

It was from the Air Force Manpower Planning. I opened it to find a letter stating it was time for a new assignment. I knew to further my career I was going to have to leave the cockpit. I loved to fly and that was a tough pill to swallow.

This was everything I had worked towards. I worked hard and I made improvements in every job I held. I was promoted early, upgraded to aircraft commander early, and held jobs usually reserved for those with higher rank. My wife Martha and I had a nice house. She was working as a certified x-ray technician, and I was being considered for a very important position. Yet, there I was sitting at my desk wondering what was missing. I *should* have been happy. I *should* have been satisfied. That is what I kept telling myself.

I was an Air Force Officer and pilot. I came from humble beginnings, and I had accomplished much more than anyone else in my family. I had traveled the world, been to war, and flown faster than the speed of sound.

Am I selfish? Am I greedy?

I wanted to be happy and knew there had to be more. I had to find it. It called to me and there was an ache inside of me that I had to soothe.

And there I was again, so many years later, sitting and watching the sun set, feeling the exact same way. I was having all the same thoughts and the same mental and emotional aches dominating my days and my nights.

What will make this pain go away? What will fill this hole?

This void that feels like a never-ending cycle of not feeling fulfilled. Did I need a bigger challenge? Maybe I needed a bigger goal to work towards. As I look back now, I know that I was judging myself through the only rules I knew.

I realize now that in comparing myself to others I set myself up to fail. I started to doubt whether I *deserved* happiness and success. I believed that others were happier than me. What I found was that in most cases that wasn't true, but we still judge ourselves on what we believe the truth is even if we don't know what the real truth is. That is where living by other people's rules can destroy us from the inside out. We doubt ourselves, what we want, and who we are. Even when we have it all, it isn't enough.

This void can stall us from finding our fulfillment. We start saying things like "it doesn't get any better than this" and "it just isn't meant to be." Both beliefs self-sabotage and end up limiting us. We give up and quit trying. But we can use the void to realize that there is more for us and begin to find our own set of rules.

Everyone has their set of rules. They have defined what it is to be happy, successful, and fulfilled. The question is, *Whose rules are they?* The problem is that many of us, if not all of us, are using rules that are either dictated or suggested by other people, society, and even marketing.

As I brought myself back to the moment, I noticed the birds were no longer singing. The sun was a brilliant orange, and the clouds were a blend of orange and pink. It looked like the sky was tie dyed, a reminder that there is so much beauty in our world. As I watched the sun slip down below the horizon, I saw my life from a different perspective.

The sky was beautiful just like my life, but I didn't want my sun to set knowing there was something else out there waiting for me.

Something was calling to me. I knew I was meant for more and I had to find what that I was. I had to find what was missing. And the sooner the better.

Chapter Two

An Ignored Crisis

*You all had to forget to develop the awareness,
understanding, and abilities for you to live a life
true to the real you and the difference you are
meant to make. And then, there comes a time for
you to awaken and remember why you chose to
come to Earth.*

The Round Table, channeled by Vince Kramer

We are constantly getting messages to wake us up to remembering and living on purpose. What do these messages look, sound, and feel like? Why is it so important that we pay attention? What if we miss an opportunity to wake up? Will there be more that will come along?

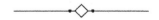

Wake-up calls are messages from the knowing part of us. That part of us is telling us it is time to live our life our way. It is time to uncover and live our unique purpose with passion. These wake-up calls start out small. We have experiences that led us to say things like, "there is something missing," "I'm not happy or fulfilled," "I've done and been everything I've been told and I'm still not happy," and "there has to be more to life." These feelings are messages that are begging us to step into the life we are meant to live.

We can choose to pay attention to these messages, these wake-up calls, or we can ignore them. You are meant to wake up, so the wake ups aren't going away. In fact, they will get bigger and bigger until they become a crisis and then we are forced to pay attention. But through free will, we may still choose not to pay attention. The smaller subtle messages are conscious wake ups. The bigger, attention-getting ones are crisis wake ups.

A wake-up call brings us to a moment of choice. Do we choose to step into being the creator of our life or do we allow ourselves to be a victim? We have free will and although we have this unique purpose, we can still choose to step into it or not. We can choose to find ways to learn and grow and support ourselves through it, or we can choose to believe life is happening *to* us and choose inaction. As we learn and grow and increase our level of awareness, we can choose to stay the same or fully move into who we truly are.

I didn't pay attention to my conscious wake ups and then had the opportunity to experience some crisis ones. There were two that I justified and basically ignored and then the one that finally caught my attention.

The first wake-up call occurred on September 11, 2001.

It was just another morning at United Airlines' multi-million-dollar training center. Being responsible for standards, I oversaw the training, qualification, and evaluation of the pilots assigned to the Airbus fleet. I made it my priority to get to work by 5 a.m. each day. By being there early, I got into the office before the day's training started which afforded me time to get most of my essential paperwork out of the way. It gave me more time to work with the instructors, evaluators, and students. I enjoyed the people-part of the job.

As I looked at the stack of essential correspondence I had just completed, I felt a sense of relief that I freed up so much valuable time for later in the day when training issues usually required more of my time and attention. I would be glad I did. That day was going to be different than any other.

I was the person responsible for maintaining training and operations standardization in our fleet, and I met regularly with the other fleets to establish standard operating procedures for the entire airline. Our meeting started at 7 a.m. and usually lasted the entire day. It was intense and important; the safety of millions of passengers depended on our actions. We were specifically chosen because we had proven we had an in-depth knowledge of our aircraft type, FAA rules and regulations, and had a general concern for giving the pilots all the possible tools to provide a safe and efficient flying experience.

The meeting that day would never get officially started. I was walking down a mostly deserted hallway, sharing a hello or good morning with the people I met on my way to the conference room. It was five minutes to seven and I was walking at a good pace to get to the meeting on time. As I passed Joel, one of the instructors at the center, he told me an airplane had just flown into the World Trade Center.

I couldn't believe it.

I pictured in my mind: a Cessna 172 or a similar type of small aircraft with an inexperienced pilot crashing into one of the towers. Accidents are a regular occurrence in general aviation, although crashing into the World Trade Center would be quite unusual even for any type of aircraft. I gave it little thought.

About half of the scheduled attendees were in the room when I arrived. The normal pleasantries were being exchanged among those already there. I noticed Paul, the 747-fleet representative on the phone. I could see by his wide-open eyes and sullen face there was something wrong. All of my attention was on him. He wasn't saying a word, just nodding his head up and down more rapidly than you would expect for someone who was just being agreeable.

There was something wrong and it wasn't good.

I uncharacteristically yelled across the room to turn on the TV. The conference room was outfitted with the most modern technology. It was the alternate crisis center if there was an incident or accident with a United Airlines aircraft. There were several TVs scattered throughout the room and a few of the pilots moved to turn on a TV. They weren't moving fast enough for Paul, and he screamed with a sense of urgency, "Turn on the TV now!"

I could see the panic on his face. He was bright red; the adrenaline was flowing. I immediately flashed back to my quick conversation with Joel, *the World Trade Center.*

Just as the realization hit me, the TV came on and there was the North Tower in flames.

That was no Cessna 172.

The volume on the TV was high, and the room fell silent; we all just listened. There was still much speculation from the news reporter as he mostly rambled a list of possibilities, but no definitive information. Everyone in the room was glued to one of the TVs tuned to other stations.

The pilot instructor side of me kicked in as I started to run several scenarios through my head all at once, and I knew every other pilot in the room was doing the exact same thing.

Was it birds, engine failures, incapacitation? What type of airplane? How much fuel? Which airline?

There were so many questions, yet there was no time to be upset and worried. The instinct and personality of a professional airline pilot is to be in control and calm. On top of that, my job focused on safety and understanding what might have happened and the options around the findings.

Then live on TV, I watched with everyone in that room and thousands of people around the world as the second plane hit the South Tower.

It was a big airplane, probably a 767, and it looked like United colors. The airplane from the camera's vantage point looked like it had the all-too-familiar United tulip on the tail.

I felt the adrenaline rush through my body as it and my senses were on hyper alert. I started taking notes of everything I saw and could remember about the tragedy I just witnessed. My hands were steady, and my thoughts were clear. I had been trained both as a military pilot and as a commercial airline pilot to remain in control, calm. I had been trained to take in as much information as possible before drawing any conclusions. It wasn't just the training, people called to the flying world have a personality they created that thrives in this environment.

This was no coincidence. There was something very wrong, and I wondered if there would be more aircraft and more landmarks. I packed up everything I had taken to the meeting and started back to my work area. I knew that plans were already being made and I wanted to make myself more available. I rushed through the halls towards my office. Everyone was either completely quiet or talking incessantly. Everyone handles emergency differently, and this was a national—or perhaps international—emergency. We were still trying to determine if United aircraft were involved. If they were United aircraft, what type? The pace was fast and forced; it looked like ants scattering but each knowing their job and doing it.

I made my way directly to my boss's office. His assistant was sitting behind his desk. I learned my boss was already on his way to the room I was just in. Both the crisis center at the United World Headquarters in Chicago and the alternate crisis center in Denver had been activated.

The man behind the desk shared the news we were afraid of: The second aircraft was a United jet.

We still weren't sure what aircraft type, although it was believed to be a Boeing 767. Ray was doing a great job of coordinating us in the fleet in accomplishing all the checklists that all needed to be done in case of a crash. The stress was obviously getting to him; he was talking so fast that he was getting confused on what he had already said.

He instructed me to go home and pack a bag. If it was an Airbus, I'd be deployed to the crash site. "Take your manuals and your computer, you'll need them," he instructed.

"On my way, I'll stay in touch," I acknowledged.

Just as I stepped out the door, he yelled after me, "Pack for a couple of weeks, and please be careful." I waved back to him and appreciated the concern.

As I made my way to the parking lot, I passed several people on the way. Each of them displayed the same look of shock that I felt in my heart. I was concentrating on the task at hand and kept wondering if there would be more. At the same time, the thoughts of what was to come in the aftermath had already made their way into my head. Just as I would in the cockpit, I channeled my energy to the task at hand and compartmentalized, shutting out what wasn't pertinent to the crisis.

It was a beautiful day in Colorado. Traffic was moving at about 65 miles an hour; it was a typical Tuesday morning. One would never know the country was falling under attack on the east coast. And like most everyone else, I was glued to a news source, but I had a mission. I wondered how many were still unaware of what was happening to our country, to our world.

I finally realized I hadn't called Martha. She knew I was not flying that day, but I knew she must be worried about me. I tried to call her several times, but the airwaves were taxed to their capacity; I couldn't get through. Mixed among my thoughts of what may have happened, I wondered about how this might have been different. *I might have been the captain on one of these flights. What would I have done? What would happen to Martha?* As I realized I was letting myself slip into the what ifs, I shut it down immediately. I had a job to do. I drove the remaining twenty minutes in silence thinking about the families of the flight crews, people on the planes, and those in the buildings on the ground.

I spent the rest of the morning packing and preparing for a trip to New York or Pennsylvania, the two known crash sites for United jets. It seemed there were only going to be four incidents.

I was left alone with my thoughts. Just me and the TV, just me and the phone. I sat down in the green plaid chair that overlooked the city below through the large glass windows on the east side of the house. I could see the airport, void of any aircraft in the sky. I began to wonder how our lives were going to be affected. The adrenaline must have worn off, and I drifted off to sleep—nightmares crept in, a sub-conscious reminder of what might have been.

The phone startled me awake and my heart immediately began pounding in my chest. I could feel it beat in every part of my body. It felt like my head would explode with the rush of adrenaline in my body. When I answered the phone, it was Martha. I was strong for her and for me just like I was supposed to be. I shared what I knew and what the possibilities might look like. The shock set in, and I began to shake.

"If I don't tell you often enough," I professed, "I love you."

We agreed she would come home as soon as she could in case I had to leave to report to an accident site investigation for United. We said goodbye with another "I love you." I noticed my hand and my entire body shaking as I hung up. I was sure it was still the adrenaline. The phone didn't stop ringing all afternoon and it continued well into the night. Hundreds of people called to make sure I was safe. It was the most loved I had ever felt in my life. *What if it would have been me*, the thoughts ran through my head yet again.

I came to learn that the captain of United Flight 93, the one that crashed in Pennsylvania, was a friend of mine and a fellow evaluator at the training center. I actually flew that flight one week prior. *Seven days earlier and it could have been me on the airplane that crashed in that field in Pennsylvania.* We still don't know exactly how or when my friend Jason and his co-pilot died that day, but we know they went down fighting.

That September day was a wake-up call for all of us. For me, it was a moment of choice. I knew I wanted to live my life differently. I wanted to experience life the way it is meant to be experienced. I wanted to tell people I love them and share just how much they mean to me every day.

But just like everyone else, I forgot.

I went back to the same old life in less than a year. Despite the changes in security and procedures that reminded me of that fateful day every time I flew, I forgot I wanted to live life differently. I forgot I wanted to live life fully.

We all have a tendency to look at these wake-up calls from the perspective that it is something that happened to us. Or in my case, I looked at it as something that happened to someone else. Even though it did affect me directly, I ignored this moment of choice and justified it all in my head. I followed grandpa's rules and pushed ahead trying to find what was missing *his way*, because I didn't know any other way.

Chapter Three

Grandpa's Rules

*Only you have your answers and can choose
your path. Others will want to share their way,
but only you can see what is to be learned from
them and implemented in your life. You are the
creator of your reality.*

The Round Table, channeled by Vince Kramer

Most of us learn from the most influential people in our lives;
they introduce us to the world and teach us how to show up
in it. Our parents or primary caregivers spend the most time with us
and have the biggest effect. It only makes sense that their parents,
our grandparents, also play a role in how we look at and experience
the world. The list grows and expands from there to teachers,
religious leaders, coaches, and other family members and the way
they influence us with their beliefs and perceptions of life and how
to live it.

Each of these people developed their own personal set of rules for
living. They learned and accepted rules from others, developed
from their perceptions of what happened in their lives, and from the

norms of society. Unfortunately, most of these rules are handed down from generation to generation. No one questions them. We accept these rules because in most cases they come from people who are older and more experienced and from the people who care about us the most who are truly responsible for our safety and well-being. Many of the rules have been handed down based on societal, gender, religious, and regional beliefs.

Because of the roles these people play in our lives and the fact that they are the ones who are supposed to keep us safe and love us, we feel that they know best, and we mostly accept the rules or beliefs without question. We take these beliefs and make them our set of rules.

Don't get me wrong, these rules are taught to us because the person who is sharing the rule wants the best for us. They don't want us to experience the pain or disappointment that they experienced. They have been using these rules to become who they are and to show up how they have been showing up. And they believe it has worked well for them. If it worked well for them (or at least okay), we believe it has to work for us.

We also develop our own rules or beliefs around our perceptions and interpretations of our experiences growing up, especially in our early years. We wanted to be loved, safe, accepted, and fed. We noticed the reactions of the people who were responsible for providing one or more of these very important and essential things to our actions. Then we decided if those actions were acceptable or not, right or wrong, and they became part of our rules. We chose a set of rules for our life based on a child's perception of adults' actions.

Let me give you a simple example. Sally was an intelligent and very excited child. Everything was magical to her. She couldn't wait to share her experiences with her parents at the end of the day. As soon as her father walked through the door, she would go on and on. Her father was never in a good mood when he returned from work. He would listen for so long and inevitably end up screaming at Sally that she talked too much. He would tell her that no one wants to hear all about her day. Because she didn't get the response she wanted from her dad—love—she believed she was wrong, and she chose a rule or formed a belief that no one wanted to hear what she had to share. She stopped sharing her thoughts and feelings.

But what if each of us comes to this earth with a life that we alone are meant to live and experience? How could we ever uncover it and live it if we are doing everything someone else's way, living by *their* rules. By living someone's set of rules, we can become just like them. But we are meant to be who *we* are. We need to choose our rules, so we can live our life our way.

I've been successful all my life. It hasn't mattered whether in school, the military, corporate, or the flying world. I have gone beyond succeeding. Much of it had to do with the way I was taught. I learned early in my life, from three of the most influential men, about achieving, competing, and succeeding. My grandfather was the most vocal. He wasn't my real grandfather, but my mom's stepdad. He taught me to always compete, to be aggressive, and to never settle. He taught me to stop dreaming, and he clearly defined for me what it meant to be a man, according to his terms. I also learned other rules like big boys don't cry, children should be seen and not heard, money doesn't grow on trees, and only the strong survive.

The rules didn't feel right, but who was I to question the adults? They knew best and I strove to follow these rules even though they didn't feel right to me. I stopped questioning them and made them my own. Even though I followed them, I always knew there was something missing. I just didn't know what it was.

I was a good student and learned very easily. I followed all the rules, especially my grandfather's because I wanted him to accept me and to be proud of me.

I became very successful. I got my bachelor's and master's degrees, excelled in sports, received many honors in the military, successfully owned several businesses, held directorate level corporate positions, and flew as both a military and a major airline pilot. By society's standards, in fact by *my* standards, I had lived a very successful life. But no matter what I accomplished, there was always something missing. Because of how I was taught, I thought the answer was to strive for more, be more, and to achieve something more. The answer was out there somewhere but searching for it had made me numb on the inside.

I didn't have just my achievements, I also had *things* that were proof. I had a spectacular house in the Colorado mountains, a beautiful wife, a great job, and a big bank account. I thought I was happy. By the rules I learned as a child, I was everything I was supposed to be. I was happy by everyone else's rules.

I followed all the rules and did exactly what I was supposed to do. At least, I thought I was achieving everything I believed brought everyone else happiness, but there was something missing.

It all started about the time I was seven. First, it was grades and then it was my performance in sports. Nothing was ever good enough; as a seven-year-old, I wasn't good enough. I vividly remember the time when I was ten years old. I had been trying to please my grandfather for years. He had trophies in his basement from his achievements in sports, and I stood in front of his big wooden plaque every chance I got admiring his baseball glove surrounded by medals of every shape, size, and color. The only place I had ever seen that many medals was on the chest of a general, and I held this man in that esteem. I know now it was because his love and acceptance were so evasive.

I was doing well in school and sports, and I wanted his approval. I was staying at my grandparents' house for the weekend because grandpa needed help in the yard. I heard him come home from work, and I suddenly put everything back just the way I found it.

He wouldn't be happy that I had all his memorabilia out. I ran upstairs to share the news that I knew would finally gain his approval. I knew it would make him proud this time. It—well actually, I—had never been good enough, but this time would be different, I just knew it.

I found him on his throne, a large, brown leather chair that vibrated. It was one of those really big ones that leans back and swivels. He had a tall, oversized end table right next to it where he kept his glasses and his drink. He was sitting back deep into the chair, reclined with his feet in the air. He had his shoes off, just relaxing in his undershirt relieving the tensions of his day. He already had his three fingers of whiskey over three cubes of ice. I had been here before, so I surveyed his mood before I ever took a step into the room.

All seemed fine; the curtains were open, and the sun was shining in the window. I mentally went through the checklist in my mind. He wasn't trying to nap. The TV was off, so I wouldn't interrupt the game. I thought I was safe, but I still glanced at my grandma to make sure it was alright to interrupt him. She nodded and gave me a quick smile.

I walked straight to his chair with a big smile on my face and handed him my grade card. I was proud of it, and I wanted him to see it. Then I sat in my grandma's chair that was right next to his on the other side of the table. It was much smaller and made of cloth, not leather like his. It didn't recline, but it did rock. I was sitting on the very edge of the cushion and unconsciously rocking as I waited for my grandpa to say something. I had received all A's again. All A's for all four quarters, *he has to be proud. He just has to*. It seemed like forever waiting for him to say something. The old clock on the wall was counting off the seconds loudly, tick, tock, tick, tock. It and he were making this wait unbearable.

"This is good," he said. The smile on my face in that moment had to brighten the entire room. I was too quick to receive the acceptance, there was a *but*.

"But you know that school is easy now and you'll have to be better. You will need to take harder courses if you ever want to make something of yourself," he quickly added after my display of being accepted. "Only the smartest people get the good jobs, and you will need to be first in your class. You will have to work much harder than you do now," was his retort to my smile.

This was a mild lecture, I still felt like I had pleased him. And then he continued, "I'm not sure you have the genetics to be number one in your class."

This is my step-grandfather, my real grandfather died when my mom was only two years old. *Oh yea*, I say in my mind, *I'll show you*. This wasn't the first time he had put my parents down. His relationship with my mom was strained at best, and I don't remember him ever treating my dad very well.

I wasn't finished. I had more to show him. This one he couldn't find fault or judgment in. I was sure of it. Hoping I could get some level of approval without stipulation, I handed him a clipping out of last night's newspaper. He had probably already seen it, but I wanted to be sure. It was an article with the summary of my little league team's game earlier in the week. I played first base for the team that was sponsored by the local police department. The article was titled, "Kramer leads Fremont Police to 4-0 start." I made the headline for an undefeated team. The HEADLINE! In the article there was a sentence just about me. "Vince Kramer made several critical defensive plays and went 4 for 4 at the plate with one home run and a walk."

I watched his face and saw no change. I was about to get out of that chair and leave the room, go to the safety of the kitchen and my grandmother. Too late.

"What happened this one time you didn't get a hit?" he started. "How you show up on the field is how you show up in life. Do you want to come up short? The people who are perfect... they will get the good jobs. They will get the money. You've got to give it your all. What were you thinking?" He was referring to the walk. I should have got another hit instead of walking. I didn't have a choice; the pitcher hadn't thrown anything I could hit. But that didn't matter.

I was doing everything to hold back the tears. I knew the rules: Big boys don't cry; if you want to be a man you've got to act like one. I'd heard them all before. I just wanted this man to be proud of me. Just once. The litany continued. There was nothing new, but that didn't mean it hurt any less.

"First place isn't good enough if you want to make it in this world. Your friend on your team wants to be better than you and he'll do whatever it takes." Without taking a breath he continued to belittle me, to teach me his rules of life, his way to be a man.

"I hate you," I said, unable to hold back any longer as I made a motion towards the kitchen.

I saw my grandmother and knew although she could never come to my rescue, at least there was some refuge. He knew I was leaving. He had to get the last barbs out of his mouth before I was gone. It was the spear that penetrated my heart.

"You better change boy, toughen up, or you are going to end up just like your father," he yelled after me.

I continued running right past my grandmother, out the door into the garage and into the backyard. I hated him. I hated him for making me want to cry so I would prove I was weak. I hated him for not believing in me. I hated him for what he said about my dad. I would show him, I would be the best. I would be successful. My tears ran like a waterfall down my face. My chest ached with a broken heart. At that moment I started to compete to be the best. I didn't compete with others, I competed against myself. A competition I could never win. I would be successful, but there would always be something missing. It would be forty years before I found it.

Moment of Reflection

We believe that because people are older, more mature, act like they know it all, or are our teachers that they know what is best for us. We all want to be loved and accepted especially by those who are closest to us. Unfortunately, we learn to follow their way and leave ours behind. We sacrifice our own knowing to live up to the demands of those who think they know best for us.

We can spend a lifetime trying to please them as we lose ourselves. When they share what we should expect in life or how we are going to turn out, we start to learn that we are limited or that our station in life has been predetermined. When we live by their rules, we live some semblance of their life, and it leaves us lost and unfulfilled. Our life is limited.

Our parents, grandparents, and teachers teach us their way or the accepted way. They are doing their best, but they pass on their beliefs, and we tend to hold on to the limiting ones.

The good news? Beliefs aren't real. We can choose to accept and follow beliefs that empower us instead of the ones that limit us.

Chapter Four

Moments of Choice

*You are constantly getting messages or
promptings to awaken you to the real you and
the unlimited possibilities that are available to
you. You must watch and listen for them being
prepared to take action.*

The Round Table, channeled by Vince Kramer

I basically ignored my opportunity to wake up and kept following
grandpa's rules, pushing and achieving, occasionally trying to
find out what was missing from my life. Not long after, another
wake-up call occurred. This one was more personal.

September 11th did change the world in many ways. It certainly
changed mine. The airline was shrinking—fast. I was holding on
with every bit of hope I could muster in keeping my job. With
shrinking comes furloughs or layoffs and I was not sure how deep
they were going to go. I noticed the stress set in. What was I going
to do? What if the airline didn't survive? Every employee was
feeling the tension. Every employee knew that life was going to be
different.

United Airlines announced that they had filed for Chapter 11 bankruptcy just sixteen days before Christmas in 2003. My world was about to come crashing down just like it would for every one of the 80,000 employees in varying degrees. I was shocked. The feeling of despair rained over me, and I quickly took a victim role. How could they do this to me? I had worked so hard and had been so loyal.

I held on to the hope of surviving in the company. While I kept a job, I lost my understanding of security, work ethic, loyalty, dedication, success, and much more. How could this happen to me? How could this happen to us? How could they do this?

In the aftermath of this business move, I lost my pension and my stock options. I found myself still employed, but over the next two years, I took a 60 percent pay cut with reduction in wages and position displacements into lower-paying jobs. I was still alive. I was happily married, and I was healthy. All of these were very important. It was another opportunity for me to decide how I wanted to live my life.

But, once again, I didn't pay attention. This time I was hearing my father's voice in my head. It was my job as a man to take care of my family. There was no time to try and figure out why this happened or to realize that this was a moment of choice calling me to something more. The wake-up call was big and loud, yet I turned my attention to finding a way to replace my income and support my family the way we had become accustomed.

I bought a business that consisted of three pretzel stores based in local malls. This was going to be my answer to funding my retirement. About the same time I bought the stores, Dr. Atkins published his book on low-carb eating. The timing could not have been worse. For the next three years I suffered, working long hours every week, just to keep the stores profitable.

Little did I know I was contributing to the next wake up, the one that would finally get my attention.

When I bought the stores three years earlier, it seemed it was the perfect solution to the loss of my United retirement. Martha and I were excited about our find. We believed that the structure in place was sound, and we would need to put very little effort into them. That bubble was burst early, and Martha decided that she wasn't interested in being involved with the business or the employees. It was my job to support the family and provide a retirement, so I took on the added workload. It almost killed me. The stress kept me up at night, and I was tired all the time. I wasn't mean to anyone, but I was definitely unavailable. My mind was occupied with all the *shoulds*, *musts*, and *could haves*. And I didn't have a choice. Martha left me to run these businesses and work my full-time job.

It had been two weeks since we sold our pretzel stores, and I was feeling really good. For three years, I worked up to ninety-five-hour weeks trying to keep my head above water. The drive home was relaxing, I was feeling good, no phone calls, no catastrophes, and no employees. I felt like I finally had an opportunity to breathe and to take my life back.

With the stores sold, I felt like my old self. I caught myself singing along to the Garth Brooks song on the radio one cool August day. There must have been a cold front coming through. I had the windows down in my truck and the wind blowing through my hair gave me a sense of freedom that I hadn't had for a while. Martha hadn't been feeling very well and that had added to my worries.

Having sold the pretzel stores, I was able to get back to a routine. I was going to work early so I could make the drive home before traffic got too bad. I had a tendency towards road rage which the stress of the businesses and Martha's health had exacerbated. It was getting better since the sale, but it was best for me to avoid the heavier traffic. This was a great drive, and I was on top of the world.

I opened the garage door as I pulled into the driveway. There was Martha's car parked in its normal spot. *That's strange*, I thought to myself. She normally got home several hours later than I got home that day. I hoped there was nothing wrong.

As soon as I walked through the door and into the house and closed the door behind me, I called out to her. "Martha, where are you? Is everything alright?"

I made my way out of the small hallway that led from the garage into the main living area. I saw her standing at the corner of the L-shaped island that separated the kitchen from the great room. It was hard to see her face because she was backlit by the afternoon August sun glaring through the window behind her.

I could barely make out her facial features. It was obvious that there was something very wrong. We had been married for over twenty years and I knew her very well. As I began to suggest we sit down, she started to cry. She actually began to sob. I stepped toward her, and she took a step back. The sobbing was getting more intense. Every time I took a step towards her, she moved backward away from me. I was starting to panic.

"What's wrong?" I asked her.

She couldn't talk. The tears were rolling down her face and her lips were quivering uncontrollably. I noticed my body rocking back and forth. I was confused and didn't know what to do. I had to get her to talk to me.

"Are you okay? Is there something wrong?" I asked with no response. Nothing! "Did something happen to you today?" She shook her head no. All the possibilities were going through my head. Was it her job? One of our friends? It could be anything.

I didn't know what else to try so I yelled, "Stop!" at the top of my voice.

It was enough to scare her into some semblance of control and she blurted out, "I really screwed up our lives," before she continued to cry uncontrollably.

I was still very concerned, but I'd narrowed it down. I found myself holding my head with both hands. I prided myself in being able to handle any situation, but I was lost. We were both out of control at that point, and I couldn't help either of us. I fired off another set of questions.

"Were you in an accident?" She shook her head no.

"Did you hurt someone?" Another no.

"Did you get fired?" Yet another no. A minimal response to any of the questions.

And then, out of my complete frustration of her unwillingness to tell me what was going on, I asked her point blank, "Are you having an affair?"

She looked directly at me, right into my eyes and I could see her heart through them. It was broken in two. Without her saying a word I had my answer.

My eyes welled up with tears and my heart broke. The pain moved instantly to anger as my ego personality tried to protect me from this hurt that tore at my insides. I picked up a stapler off the small mail nook to my right and threw it across the room crashing into the wall twenty feet away.

"What the hell were you thinking? What is wrong with you?" I cried out half in anger, half in pain.

I wanted to hold her and make it alright. I wanted to destroy something and make me feel alright.

My entire body was shaking. It was out of control. I felt the rush of anger as heat moved up through my body like mercury in a thermometer. And then, I felt a calm overtake me like a gentle breeze.

I couldn't take my eyes off of her and she couldn't stop sobbing and murmuring she was sorry. I wanted to know all the details, and I didn't want to know anything. I was so confused and betrayed. I was torn. My emotions were changing so fast I didn't know what to think, feel, or do. I was a wreck. I had no control in one moment and then I was calm and subdued in the next. I continuously moved from being subdued and in control to anger and feeling unhinged and then back. How could she do this to us, to me? I knew I had been lacking when it came to being attentive and supportive because of the stores. But it was because I was working all those hours in a business she agreed to be part of and she stranded me with. I did it for her and us. And then I found out she was with another man when I was killing myself.

I resigned myself to the fact that nothing was going to be solved that night. My head felt like it was going to explode, my heart already had. I decided to go to bed. As I stood in front of the mirror, I saw the reality of my pain reflected back at me. My bloodshot eyes and tear-stained face showed me the rejection and hopelessness I felt. I'd never felt that alone. I finally fell asleep when I just couldn't think anymore.

When I opened my eyes and looked at the empty bed beside me, I had to admit to myself, *This isn't a dream. It is real.* I was going to do whatever it took to fix this problem. Life wasn't going to stop for us. I wouldn't let it. I got dressed and went to work. I knew how to compartmentalize. I did it every time I closed the cockpit door. I closed the cockpit door to my heart, and no one was the wiser.

Martha wanted time to herself and to think. I wanted to talk things out. We were at odds and our conversations led us nowhere. She moved out and it was two months before any talking began.

Four months later, on Valentine's Day, we went for a walk at a local park. About twenty minutes into our walk, we were still talking about meaningless things. I was hoping to find a way, any way, back to the old us. I was nervous, making sure every word was perfectly chosen. It was obvious we were both walking on eggshells. It had become much more hospitable, neither of us showing any anger. From my side, the anger was gone. I felt it was gone for her too. She was sad and I wanted to hold her. I wanted to tell her it would be okay, but I no longer believed it myself. I was going through the motions without much hope.

I glanced over and noticed Martha crying. The tears quietly dropped off her cheeks. We sat down at the base of a tree. Side by side, we each experienced the pain of the moment.

We both knew.

I let her cry, and I allowed myself to feel the emptiness that was happening inside me.

"Are you that unhappy?" I asked.

"Yes," she managed to express.

"And you think you can be happy not married to me?" I continued.

"I don't know that, but I have to try," she responded.

"Then, I'll agree to a divorce. It's not what I want, but I love you, and I won't stand in your way," I said with all sincerity.

We sat there softly crying together. We both knew that it was the end of our twenty-one years together. I was devastated but I couldn't let it show. She deserved to be happy. So did I. We would both be fine. But at that moment, I was empty—depleted. There was no more fight left in me. We walked to our cars in silence.

I had been getting messages and wake-up calls for a long time. Each time, I just didn't pay attention. And I'm not alone. We all miss messages that are meant to give us direction, wake us up, and help us on the journey. We believe we are victims when bad things happen in our lives instead of understanding they are meant to get our attention. We discount our knowingness as a child and allow ourselves to be taught or told how life is or should be.

With my divorce, something finally got my attention. I knew life could be different, I wanted to find out what had been missing. I wasn't going to let anything stop me, and I certainly wasn't going to wait around and wait for something else to happen.

Chapter Five

Life Meant to Live

Your journey is yours and yours alone and you
see glimpses of it or reminded of it often. Even if
you choose to ignore these reminders, you will
feel the pull or the calling to discover and
create that life. You chose it and others will help
you remember it.

The Round Table, channeled by Vince Kramer

I have come to believe that we all have a life that we are meant to live. Not a life that is predetermined, but one that is meant to make a difference in the world. When I was younger and through most of my adult life, I believed that there was a plan for us and everything that happened was pre-orchestrated to make sure we lived that plan. Some might call it fate or God's plan but, I believed that there wasn't much choice in the matter. I guess I really believed that I was along for the ride.

But the way I looked at life then and what I believe now is quite different.

Here's what I think. Everyone came into this world with a reason, or mission. Because of that, we have agreements with other energies, other souls, to develop everything needed to live this mission. We have a natural blueprint which includes the jobs, the people, the process of life. If we don't design our life around it, we are never going to be completely successful, content, or happy because we can't or won't fulfill our mission. We call living our mission in this way, the "life we are meant to live." We are finally able to make the difference we are meant to make and solve the problems we are meant to solve.

We are all energy; in fact, everything is energy. And, what if as an energy we chose our life before we were born? As that energy, we came to experience the highest and lowest vibrations of the energy stream we chose. We came to live a purpose, make a difference, and help others to do the same. We actually came with a mission, or what I like to call *a divine intent*. We came to live the life we are meant to live. Even if we think it isn't going to get any better than it is right now, there will be a time we wake up to more.

What if we chose the time and place we were to be born in support of bringing our energy and divine intent into the world in a way that supported us living the life we are meant to live? What if we chose our parents to help us develop everything we needed to live that life? And along with our parents, there were our grandparents, religion, school, friends, and family? Everything we needed to develop ourselves fully in living on purpose.

What if we came into this world fully knowing all of this, but had to forget in order to live life in a way that prepared us to live our divine intent and the life we were meant to live? We had to forget so the circumstances in our lives would make us uncover, discover, and develop a unique set of gifts and talents to live in a way that allowed us to live the life that we chose.

In my research and interviewing many people that remember knowing their purpose even when they were younger, I've come to believe that all of these *what ifs* that I suggested above are true. I had to be reminded several times that I knew my divine intent at a young age. I spoke of it often before "forgetting" it because I'd learned to live by grandpa's rules. I was reminded of it from time to time. The most memorable was a reminder by my grandmother.

Most of the family was there in the hospital. Some were in Grandma's room, others—with me—were in the sparse, magazine-strewn waiting room haunted by the energy of despair. We waited for her to die, and while I wasn't afraid of death and dying, I wondered if the family could survive the loss. What would happen?

It was okay with me that I wasn't in the room with her. I wasn't afraid of death. I had seen it up close. When I was about ten, I found the neighbor's dad lying dead at the edge of the garden. Although it was surprising, it didn't bother me seeing death. My parents made sure I attended the showing at the funeral home so I could have a different image of him. It was worse for me to see everyone crying and him covered in make up looking like an old mannequin.

The last time I was in her room, Grandma didn't look so good, and I wasn't sure if she even wanted anyone to see her that way. I was seventeen years old and loved her very much. Along with my three younger brothers I had spent some time with her a couple days before. It was just the five of us. She was very lucid when we were with her, and we all got a chance to share our "I love yous" and "I'll miss yous." I wasn't sure I cared to see her last few minutes and preferred to remember our last interaction. As I looked around the waiting room, I sensed others were feeling the same. Each person was handling it their own way. My brothers at least pretended to watch the TV.

I noticed my mom coming down the long sterile hallway. It was lined with oxygen equipment, lab trays, and wheelchairs. I'm sure Grandma had used many of them during her long stay. As my mom acknowledged each nurse, I could see the pain of losing her mother on her face and yet, she was being extra compassionate with the nurses. Did Grandma die? Was it over? As she got closer, it was obvious my mom was coming towards me. I stood up just as she arrived at my chair. She reached out and took my hand. I didn't know what to expect.

"Your grandmother wants to see you," she whispered.

"Why?" I wondered out loud.

"I don't know but you need to come now," she said with obvious urgency.

As we walked down the hall, she continued to hold my hand, squeezing tighter and tighter. I felt her pain and let my mind wander. *What is she thinking? What is she feeling? What is it like to have a parent dying? What does my grandmother want with me?*

We arrived at the room and walked in. I immediately realized that everyone in the room was staring at me. Like me, they had no idea why I was there. Grandma mumbled something that was inaudible to me and motioned towards the door with her frail and almost lifeless left arm. It was nothing but skin and bones and the yellow coloring was very concerning. Everyone touched Grandma gently and filed out of the room one by one. Soon it was just my grandma, my mom, and me in the room. My mom squeezed my hand before letting go, gently touched my grandma's foot, and walked out of the room closing the door behind her.

My grandma held out her hand and motioned me towards her. As I walked towards the right side of the bed, I was overcome by the sadness of her dying in this room. It was plain and sterile. She was in a double occupancy room and thankfully the other bed was vacant. The walls were light green with three small photographs hanging. I hadn't even noticed them before. The only other color or sign of life in the room were the beautiful flowers from my grandmother's many friends and family.

As I grabbed her hand, I was taken by how small and frail it was. I was already well over six feet and approaching two hundred pounds. Her hand was like a child's in mine. I felt my heart ache and the tears well up in my eyes. She started to talk, and I couldn't hear or make out a single word.

"Just a second Grandma," I managed to say. I leaned over her hospital bed and got as close as I could get. My ear was just inches from her quivering mouth.

"I want to remind you of something you shared with me when you were five years old," she muttered barely at a whisper. "You told me, you wanted to help people love themselves, so they could love each other. Don't ever forget. Promise me."

I looked deep into my grandma's eyes, and I knew I was seeing her soul. I had never seen them so beautiful, even with jaundice in them. I saw the love she found so hard to express.

"Yes, I won't forget," I said through my tears.

"Promise me," she said with all the conviction she could muster from her deteriorating body and the drugs she had been given for her pain.

"I promise you." And with a knowingness, I managed to say, "Goodbye Grandma, I love you."

She squeezed my hand and mouthed the words, *I love you.*

I had just made my grandmother a promise on her deathbed. *But a promise for what?* I'm not sure what my words even meant. I understood what it meant to love others, but at seventeen, I wasn't sure what it meant to truly love myself, and I definitely had no clue why loving self was a prerequisite for loving others. Most adults I knew didn't understand that. How was a seventeen-year-old supposed to get it? Even if I did get it, how was I going to help people love themselves?

I was grateful that my grandmother had shared, but also terrified that I may never live up to a promise that felt so confusing and intimidating. Maybe that is another reason we forget. I didn't know how I could ever help people love themselves. The pressure of not knowing could deter a person from ever even trying. I felt the weight of the world on my shoulders and the pain of losing her in my heart.

The reality of where I was and who I was with set in as my mind and attention came back to my grandmother.

I left her room feeling the pain of goodbye to someone so influential in my life, knowing we would never speak again. The others were waiting just outside the door and filed back into the room as I walked away thinking only about her impending death. As I walked down the crowded hall, it seemed so empty, or maybe the emptiness was in me. I had no desire to talk to anyone, so I looked for a chair in the corner away from everyone. I wanted to be alone. I wanted to think about what she just said and to feel the loss. I closed my eyes and ignored the world around me.

I'm not sure if I fell asleep or was deep in thought when my dad tapped me on my shoulder to tell me my grandmother was dead. She died ten minutes after our talk. I was surprised that she was gone so quickly, but I felt another surge of emotions come over me. Of course, the sadness of loss was one, but the other was gratitude for the gift she had just given me, a reminder of what I knew my purpose to be on this Earth. I held this time with her as sacred. It was over thirty-three years before I shared this story or even her words with anyone.

Moment of Reflection

As I look back now, there were many times when something was said, or something happened, that I didn't pay attention to or chose to forget. And I'm not alone. Many times, we don't pay attention to the things that happen in our lives that are trying to get our attention. We have been taught that things happen *to* us instead of *for* us. It is actually truer to say that things happen *because* of us.

We all came to this Earth with a unique purpose and a life that we are meant to live. We tend to discount our knowingness—especially the knowingness we had as a child. Of course, we wouldn't believe in something if the adults around us didn't. And why would we ever listen to the messages to remind us? Why would we ever pay attention or take action?

Chapter Six

A Teacher Appears

*You all are constantly being given messages and
co-creations from the non-physical part of you,
your higher self that is connected to all there is.
These messages and co-creations are helping
you to rediscover and remember the real you
and why you are here.*

The Round Table, channeled by Vince Kramer

When I share that we have a life we are meant to live, I'm referring to living our unique purpose and making the difference we are meant to make. Our Unique Purpose consists of three parts, Quintessence, our Gift, and our Divine Intent. *Quintessence* is the real and concentrated essence of who we are. *Gift* is the unique combination of gifts and talents, as well as the process one uses to share them. *Divine Intent* is a person's mission or why.

For us to live our unique purpose, we need to forget who we are and why we are here long enough to develop our Gift—the gifts, talents, and process to share our Unique Purpose with the world. When it is time to start remembering what we forgot, our wake-up calls help us get familiar with and move along the path of our journey. Our journey is to live our purpose, our Divine Intent. When our Gift is developed enough for us to fully step into living our Divine Intent, it is time to remember who we are and why we are here.

We are the only ones that know the answers to what the three parts of our Unique Purpose are, but most of the time, we need help finding them. Unfortunately, no one is going to show up at our door someday and give us the answers. But, when it is time and a person is ready, they will get the calling, and help will appear. When I was ready, Jack Canfield appeared to help me find my mission.

There I was sitting in the midst of 400 plus people in Scottsdale, Arizona. The entire hotel was beautiful, especially the massive ballroom. The southwest flair was very pleasing, and I was allowing myself to just relax and enjoy the experience. I was starting day two of Jack Canfield's multi-day Breakthrough to Success workshop. Without exaggeration, the last ten months had been the toughest and most stressful of my life. I hadn't slept. I was nervous and edgy. I couldn't concentrate, and I was on pins and needles all the time. I was able to maintain the status quo at work. The break I had at the workshop was needed and extremely good for me. I was surrounded by very positive, happy people ready to have their lives transformed by America's Success Coach.

I wouldn't have been there without Martha. When she first told me she was unhappy and wanted a divorce, she was depressed and going through a very difficult time in her life. I was devastated because I couldn't help her. She had moved out of the house two months earlier because she wasn't sure she wanted to be married any longer. I was still trying diligently to find a way to get us back together. I wanted to help her and us any way I could. The answer would come.

Throughout much of our marriage, Martha was a dedicated listener to an audio series called *Self-Esteem and Peak Performance* by a man I had never heard of before, Jack Canfield. This was before Jack became a household word because of the Chicken Soup for the Soul series. One morning in early December, I received a marketing email. I normally don't open this type of email, but I noticed Self-Esteem in the synopsis of the email. For some reason, I clicked on the email without giving it a second thought. It was marketing an upcoming workshop by the author of the very *Self-Esteem and Peak Performance* program that Martha had listened to at least twenty times. This was the answer, I was sure of it. I clicked on the link with an excitement that I hadn't felt in some time. This was the perfect Christmas present for Martha, and I knew it would help bring us back together. I didn't care what the price was. She had already turned down any possibility of counseling, and I saw this as a very viable alternative.

I clicked on the link to sign up without any hesitation. I signed Martha up first, filling in all her information before clicking the Buy Now button. Next, I filled in all of my information and purchased another ticket. It was still six months away, but I knew we would still be together, I just knew it.

Two weeks after making the purchase, I gave her the gift of the workshop as her Christmas present. By the smile on her face, I could tell she was very excited about it. At least, until she learned I was going also. She went from joy and excitement to being shut down and resistant. Her reluctance was heartbreaking. I was able to convince her to give it some time before she made any decision. Any hope I had was destroyed by her reaction, but I wasn't ready to give up. Two months later when I agreed to the divorce she wanted, I told her I was going to the event, and I thought she should also go. She didn't answer one way or the other at that moment, but it was obvious she wasn't thrilled by the idea when she rolled her eyes and shook her head. She actually said she wasn't going if I went. I was sorry she felt that way, but I had to go. I had to find what was missing in my life.

And six months later and after the divorce, I was sitting in a room with people who were all strangers a few days earlier, but who would remain lifelong friends. We were preparing for a guided meditation that Jack had been telling us about since the workshop started. I had never meditated before, and I wasn't sure I knew what *guided meditation* meant. I was about to find out and I was about to have my life changed forever. I must admit I was scared. What if I couldn't do it? What if it was strange and I freaked out or got angry? I promised myself when I got on the plane to go to the workshop, I was going to participate fully. I gave myself a verbal slap across the face and told myself to get over it. I *could* do this, and I *would* do it.

Jack asked the group if there was anyone who had never done a guided visualization or guided meditation before. I reluctantly raised my hand. As I looked around, I saw that about 20 percent of the room had their hands raised. It should have made me feel better, but it didn't. This was new and different, and I hadn't yet adopted the philosophy of trying everything and only holding on to what best served me and who I wanted to be. I was willing to be pushed, but not too far out of my comfort zone. I felt safe in that group, so I thought *Let's just do this*. Jack then described what we were going to do. I trusted him, but I kept thinking *Let's just do this before I want to quit.*

Eventually the lights dimmed, and soft rhythmic music began to play in the background. My eyes darted across the room to see what I was supposed to be doing. Most everyone was sitting back in their chair with their eyes closed. I felt like a child learning something for the very first time. Like everyone else, I slid my workbook under my chair and turned my attention to the stage where Jack was sitting on a barstool.

In a soft, soothing voice he instructed us to close our eyes. I was sure the combination of the music, the calmness in his voice, and closing my eyes was responsible for the way my body was beginning to feel relaxed. He had us imagine a ball of white light at our feet. At first it was difficult, but it became much easier the more I relaxed with each suggestion he shared. By the time he moved the white ball of light through our bodies three times, I was the most relaxed I'd been since I could remember. I felt my body in a new and unique way. My mind was quiet, which meant I wasn't constantly thinking of different things or hearing any other voices in my head. I was relaxed, but fully aware. I realized that guided meditation was much like hypnosis.

Jack continued by asking us to imagine that we were standing in the middle of a beautiful field in nature. I was confused at first, but I didn't notice any rustling in the room. I opened my right eye briefly to see if anyone was standing. They weren't so I closed my eye and pictured myself standing in a field on a warm summer day. It all seemed so real to me.

He then asked us to imagine walking to the base of a tall, majestic mountain. When we arrived, he asked us to see a magic carpet approaching and landing at our feet. I saw it. I'm not sure I believed it, but I saw it. It was purple and gold with purple fringe. I sat down on it at Jack's suggestion, and it immediately took off.

He guided us on a magical ride on the carpet up to the top of the mountain where there was a beautiful golden temple. When I entered the temple, there was an angel waiting for me. The angel had a gift for me, wrapped in forest green and purple paper with a wide golden ribbon and matching bow. It was beautiful. The box was about sixteen inches tall, three inches wide, and three inches deep. Jack told us to open the gift. Just like when I was a little boy sitting around the Christmas tree in Ohio, I ripped the paper from the box. I opened it to find something wrapped in tissue paper. I pulled it out of the box in anticipation and unwrapped a beautiful solid gold microphone. I didn't know why a microphone. And I didn't know why it was gold.

I was questioning the validity of the meditation. and then, I heard a soft voice in my head, maybe it was the angel's that gave me the gift, saying, "What's missing in your life is you!"

I heard it loud and clear. It was so real that I opened my eyes to see if there was someone beside me whispering in my ear. I felt flush and I noticed tears running down my cheeks. I had come to the workshop to find what was missing all these years. I found that it was me. I knew that it was the truth because I felt it physically and emotionally. My chest hurt, but it was a good hurt. I couldn't stop the tears, but they were good tears.

Jack then directed us to exit the temple and to step back on the magic carpet and ride it back down to the base of the mountain, and then he slowly and gently brought us out of the guided visualization. When I opened my eyes, I recognized that everyone around me was wiping tears. I couldn't believe something I was so wary of, I wanted to do again right now. It had changed my mind and my perspective on life. In that moment, I decided I would be wide open to every experience and opportunity that came my way. And only after listening and learning, would I determine if it worked for me or not, and only then choose to keep it or let it go.

The room started to buzz with conversation and Jack asked us to quiet down. He shared that the gift in our box was a symbol for our life purpose. He asked us to take out a piece of paper and journal about it. "Don't think about what you are writing, just write," he instructed.

I'm not sure how long I wrote, and I really don't remember what I wrote about. I just felt lighter, almost like I was floating. It was like I had found a treasure—a treasure that would change the rest of my life. As I read what I wrote, an old familiar feeling came over me. I had this knowing; my body and mind were in sync. It was how I felt just before I hit a homerun or climbed in a jet. Everything was aligned. Everything was right. *I'm here on this earth to teach and to speak. I'm on track to knowing my purpose.* I knew then, I was uncovering parts of my Gift, the second of the three parts of my Unique Purpose.

Moment of Reflection

We all have a time in our life when the calling to live our purpose gets loud enough to hear, or we finally feel the pull to find it, and we start the process of discovering it. Whether it is a conscious wake up or a crisis wake up that finally gets our attention, we know that we are meant for more as we set out to learn our why, the reason we are on Earth. This usually happens in our forties, but it can happen much earlier or later.

Because we haven't been taught otherwise, we tend to look outside of ourselves to find our purpose. We know we want to make a difference and we look at how others have made a difference in our lives or the lives of others. We think that a coach, mentor, or teacher is going to be able to tell us our purpose. And we believe they can teach us to live our why.

First, let me share as I said earlier, only we know our own specific answers in finding our individual unique purpose. By trying to learn our purpose and how to live it from others, we end up living *their* purpose and not ours. It is paramount to learn our purpose and live it our way. That is how we find fulfillment and make the difference in the world the way that only we individually can. When we look to others to give us the answers, we won't fully express the magic of who we are.

Second, to fully know our unique purpose and how we are meant to make a difference in the world, we need to uncover and understand more than our why or mission. We must find the answers to the who, what, and why of us. And that is an inside job. The exciting thing is that once we have those answers, we will realize we have been living our own unique purpose all along. We will then be able to share the three parts of our Unique Purpose in a way that has an even bigger effect on those around us and makes an even bigger difference in the world.

Chapter Seven

We Meet Again

There are no mistakes or coincidences. The people you attract into your life are there to help you get on or stay on the path of your chosen journey.

The Round Table, channeled by Vince Kramer

Call it intuition or divine intervention, but we are constantly getting messages to wake us up, get us on the right path, or help accelerate us on the journey. We like to call these messages *promptings*. They are suggestions that we can use free will to choose to follow or ignore. Once acknowledged then followed, they begin to provide supportive next steps.

Promptings can come in a variety of ways. We all have our own specific combinations of how they show up. My promptings usually come as a voice in my head (something that comes into my awareness) or by something another person says to me. Promptings can also be a feeling, a dream, or a mental picture. It doesn't matter how they come. The important thing is to pay attention, notice, acknowledge, and take action on them.

Many of us stop trusting our promptings and knowingness. Others ignore them. One of the things that most of us do instead of taking action right away is run it through the filter of our brain. Because our tendency as humans is to evaluate why something won't work or can go wrong, we end up not taking action or following through. But the Universe doesn't give up on us, the messages continue to come.

Let me share an example of how the Universe sent me another prompting for something I let my head talk me out of in the past.

It had been months since I agreed to give Martha the divorce she so desperately believed she needed to find her elusive happiness. We hadn't told anyone, and we agreed it would be best. She asked that I file for divorce. I agreed to do it, but I had one request. I thought it would be helpful for both of us together to share with our friends what was happening and, most importantly, why. I felt relieved that I didn't have to explain on my own exactly what happened because I wasn't completely sure. When I thought about it at night as I fought to get some sleep, it still felt like my heart was being ripped from my chest, and I couldn't get any answers.

We visited all our closest friends and shared our decision. It wasn't easy because we both were close to all of them. We knew that our pain would be their pain. We had the toughest time sharing with the two couples we spent the most time with. We were close to them, and this divorce meant that one or both of us wouldn't be spending time with them.

The day after sharing the sad truth with the last of the two couples, Larry and Gail, my friend Larry called to check on me to see if I was alright. "Truthfully," I shared, "I'm a mess. I don't understand what has happened and much of it was a complete surprise."

Larry suggested I call Mary, a mutual friend of ours. He told me that Mary and her husband were getting a divorce and Mary may be able to help me understand our circumstances by sharing hers.

Although I thought it might be helpful, I was in no space to have that kind of conversation with anyone.

The divorce wouldn't be final for three months. I still had hope and was holding on to the possibility of getting back together. I felt like a man holding onto a rope and hanging over a cliff. One wrong move and I would plummet into the pit of despair and hopelessness. My hands were bloody, body bruised, and my arms torn with the constant pain and rejection caused by the crazy mess. I felt I could lose my grip on that rope at any moment and fall into depression. *I still don't understand, I followed all the rules, and I did what I was supposed to do to be happy. Why is this happening? Why does it hurt so much? Why doesn't anything make sense?*

Another month passed and I still remembered Larry's suggestion to call Mary. I didn't know what to do. How would she know what Martha was thinking? Why would her situation be the same as ours? It wouldn't, and I decided not to contact her.

It was important for me to keep things as normal as possible. I was doing everything that I did before with Martha, alone. The other difference was, I was mostly in pain as I did them. I found myself falling into the role of victim. Asking myself things like, *How could she do this to me? Why doesn't she love me? What did I do to deserve this?* Basically, I spent a lot of my time feeling sorry for myself and being a victim. It was destroying me from the inside out. It was destroying my self-confidence. Keeping everything as normal as possible had to include getting out in front of people and just being me, even if I had to put on a good show or answer all the questions people had.

I decided to attend one of Larry's poker games. Larry was a kind man with a gruff exterior. He was always giving by bringing people together. And his poker games were famous. He was my mirror of following the rules. All the rules society and a generation of men have told us of how we should be. His heart is huge, and his intolerance can be just as big. He and Gail hosted poker games that were more like events. As many as forty people would come together in their home for a night of friendship, fun, and competition. They invited people of all occupations and social groups. They provided a melting pot for all to have a good time and interact with other amazing people.

This night was no different except for the number of people in attendance. There were fifty or more there. Larry and Gail's home was beautifully decorated and very spacious. It was well suited for such a crowd, and it was definitely designed to entertain. I arrived a little late, at least late for someone who is always ten minutes early. I let myself in the massive double doors and stepped into the foyer. Everyone was already downstairs in the game and theater rooms. I decided to get my composure before going down the single flight of stairs to the entertainment rooms where the tables are normally set up. There were two small lights on the oak mantel over the mountain rock fireplace centered in a wall of windows looking out on the forest beyond. They cast a soft glow on the overstuffed leather furniture artfully placed throughout the simple, yet majestic space of the great room. I located a cowhide-covered ottoman in the shadows of one of the corners. I maneuvered my way over to it and sat down. It was my refuge while I prepared for what I might be about to experience.

I didn't know who would be downstairs at the game. In fact, Martha might even be there. I doubted it because I didn't see her car, but there was always a possibility. I knew for sure there would be people who knew us both, and there would be people who worked with Martha at the hospital. Larry was a surgeon and Gail was a neonatal practitioner at the same hospital where Martha worked as a radiology technician. I just needed a minute to be ready for the questions, and I felt safe in the shadows of this spacious, low-lit room.

As I finally made my way down the stairs to the poker game, I was surprised to see two overflow tables spilled out of the entertainment room. Everyone was just taking their seats and didn't see me slide past them and the overflow tables trying to be as invisible as someone 6'5" and 240 pounds could possibly be.

I walked into the room where there were four main tables set up artfully to allow plenty of room for appetizers, liquid refreshments, and nine to ten people around these professional felt-covered card tables. I felt at home and strangely safe. I made my way to Gail and Larry to say hi and to thank them for having me. They were at two different tables, and I caught Larry's eye first. Gail was at a table on the path to Larry's table and I stopped to engage her on the way to Larry. She gave me a big hug. I felt welcomed and accepted. It took some of the anxiety away. She shared that she was glad I made it and let me know that Martha wasn't coming. An immediate blanket of relief covered me. That would ensure the awkwardness of being together in the same room with this group of people would be avoided, at least for one night.

I continued towards Larry, shaking hands and giving hugs along the way. It seemed that most people didn't know or just didn't care. I still felt very self-conscious despite this reception. When I finally got to Larry, he shook my hand and gave me a hug.

"Are you doing okay?" he asks quietly. "I saved you a seat," as he points to the table to his left and my right.

I surveyed the players and noticed none of them knew about Martha and me. Coincidence? *I think not.* I took my seat at the far end of the table near the doorway. I don't suffer from claustrophobia, but it was nice to feel I had space to breathe and maybe even escape if this all got to be too much. I settled into my seat and introduced myself to six of the eight other people at the table. I said hi to the other two I'd played with before. Neither one of them worked at the hospital. They seemed generally at ease as they spoke to me. It was safe to assume there would be no divorce talk. I noticed my heart slow down a few beats per minute and my muscles relax. I'm not sure if Larry orchestrated this ensemble, but I made a mental note to thank him.

"Shuffle up and deal," Larry hollered. It was time to get serious. My ability to compartmentalize kicked in. It was time to play cards.

I love Texas Hold 'Em. It is about knowing the odds and reading the players, and I enjoy the challenge of both. It was a good evening at the tables. I won a couple big hands, and my chip stack was substantial. It was a loose group and that can be dangerous. By *loose* I mean, they are willing to bet on hands they probably shouldn't be betting on, making it difficult to predict the strength, or hopefully weakness, of their hand. I was enjoying myself for the first time in a while. I had to concentrate with the group at my table and it kept my mind busy. I finally had a genuine smile on my face after these excruciating months.

The dealer was doing a great job, and I was enjoying not having the responsibility tonight. It allowed my mind to wander. At times, I found myself thinking about the many nights Martha and I had spent here with these people playing cards. I really wasn't concentrating for several hands and thankfully came back to the game at the right time.

I felt a big win here. It was going to be a good night. I had no clue how good. Lady Luck and the Queen of Hearts were on my side!

We were getting close to a break, and I wanted to beat the crowd. I left my stack of chips at the table and excused myself. I rushed up the stairs to use the bathroom on the main level. As I stepped into the bathroom and flipped on the light, I saw someone I hadn't seen in a while: a happy me. It was good to see a smile on my face. I was as bright as the colors on the painting behind me of a child with a flower. I had some hope.

I was walking back down the stairs feeling relieved that there might be light at this long dreary tunnel when the doorbell rang.

"I got it," I yelled knowing that Larry and Gail would be okay with me answering the door. I turned and bounded back up the steps feeling lighter and happier than I had felt in months.

I'm sure there was still a huge smile on my face as I swung open the door and exclaimed, "Hi."

It was Mary and she was standing there with, who I assumed to be her youngest son, Riley. Both Mary and Riley said in unison, "Hi, how are you?"

"I'm doing okay," I admitted as I invited them both into the house, giving Mary a hug. I felt the same strong energy as the first time I met her. I couldn't help but flash back to that very moment.

Ten years before, Larry and Gail had invited Martha and me to join them on a vacation in Cabo San Lucas. They shared that there would be a fairly large number of people in their group. Arriving at the resort in early afternoon, we began to meet everyone that we didn't already know. One set of introductions would be a part of me for the rest of my life.

When I arrived at the pool to meet up with the group, Larry introduced me to the only person I didn't know that was hanging out at the pool bar. Russ was about fifteen years older than me. He shared that he and his wife Mary owned a real estate company in Colorado Springs. I remembered Larry sharing that their former neighbors Russ and Mary also had a timeshare at Cascadas. I found that Russ and I had the military and flying in common. We were talking about his Vietnam experience when he looked up and said, "There she is."

As I looked up, I saw this very attractive woman in an American flag bikini. Larry and Russ both tried to introduce me at the same time. After the confusion subsided, Larry introduced me to Mary, Russ's wife. I was uncharacteristically silent and not sure for how long. Although I found Mary to be physically attractive, something had happened that I didn't quite understand. I actually thought I felt her energy in my body. My mind was completely empty at that moment, and I couldn't grasp a single thought. At the same time, it seemed to be full of chatter that I couldn't make out no matter how hard I tried. I almost felt magnetically attracted to her like a piece of metal to a powerful electromagnet. It was like I knew her in a way people know their closest friends. It wasn't like I'd met her before. But I had this feeling that I knew all about her, like we had known each other forever. This feeling was a shock and it scared me for no other reason than this made no sense.

I finally stammered out, "It is so good to meet you. Larry has told me so much about you and your real estate business."

I quickly looked from Larry to Russ and then everyone around me. Had anyone noticed? Was it as awkward on the outside as it had been on the inside? This had never happened to me before. I was mesmerized with the feeling of wanting to be around her. What was this? It made no sense. I was confused. There was a brief conversation among the four of us. My part was pure autopilot. I didn't know what I was saying, but I felt comfortable that I wasn't saying the wrong thing. I tried to read Mary. Did she also experience this energy? From everything I could tell, she hadn't.

As Russ and Mary left, I was overwhelmed with my confusion. I worked my way out into the middle of the shark pool and dove under the water just to give myself some time to digest what had happened. I was a happily married man. Martha and I had a great relationship. I was not interested in another relationship with anyone. Yet, I had this magnetic connection. I didn't know what to think, and I especially didn't know how to talk about it with anyone. At that moment, I made the decision to stay away from her no matter what—at least until I understood what this all meant. I'd be kind and present when I was around her, but I would do everything I could to avoid a position to feel this unexplainable connection and energy again. And I did it for ten years; I stayed away.

And then, there we were, and I was experiencing the unexplainable energy yet again. I felt some guilt for not contacting her like Larry suggested. But that night, I was happy to see her because maybe she could help me understand what was happening with Martha, and I could finally relieve this pain. I was sure this was meant to happen so I could heal. Maybe I could get over the piercing pain of the pending divorce and move on.

"This is my son Riley," Mary stated proudly as she lovingly put her hand on his shoulder.

I extended my hand and as we shook hands, I said, "It is so good to meet you."

I immediately turned to Mary and rambled, "I've been wanting to call you after Larry suggested we might talk."

"I look forward to your call!" she said. She seemed sincere. "Larry mentioned to me that you might call. Did you know that I had lunch with him recently to tell him Russ and I were divorcing?"

"How did he react to your news?" I asked with genuine concern.

Mary laughed as she said, "He told me you were divorcing! He also said you were taking it hard."

"I am," I replied.

"Well, I think it's always hard to be the one on the receiving end, but you can choose to look at this very differently! I hope we will get to talk about it soon," Mary said.

As I look back now, Larry must have been a messenger for the Universe to make sure Mary and I were brought back together.

"Let's head downstairs and I'll introduce the two of you to the gang. I'm sure Larry and Gail will be happy you are here," I offered.

On the way to the stairs, the conversation stayed very casual, and I felt in that moment like I had found a friend. It felt like my heart had taken a much-needed breath for the first time in six months. I had them follow me down to the card game and introduced them to everyone we passed on the way.

Suddenly, a sense of panic came over me. Thoughts of people thinking we are together went through my head. *What will people think? Will they be talking about it behind my back? Will they ask about Martha?* There still was a chance Martha would reconsider our marriage. I told her I would do anything to make us work up until the time the judge signed the papers. I didn't want to mess up any chance of reconciling.

As we stepped into the room with the four remaining poker tables, everyone was wrapping up their short break. I yelled over the loud hum of excited chatter, "Larry, Gail, look who is here."

Mary, Riley, and I worked our way over to where Larry and Gail were standing with two of their guests who had already been eliminated from the night's tournament. As the three of them were catching up, I made my way back to my table. I used the few free minutes I had alone to get my thoughts and fears under control.

Come to find out, Mary and Riley knew very few people at the game. When the games reconvened, Mary chose to sit next to me, and Riley sat in the chair next to her. My winning hand just before the break opened up the two chairs at our table. During this next session, Mary and I talked mostly about cards and why I made the decisions I made in playing my hands. I also broke down for her what was happening with the other players. It was the perfect diversion for me, and it gave us an opportunity to start a friendship. With most of my attention on Mary, it wasn't the best for my card game though. I couldn't watch the other players as much as I wanted.

Being around Mary brought back memories of the past. I had spent years staying away from her because of the unexplainable attraction I experienced in Cabo. But the same energetic attraction was still there. And it helped me feel better about me and my life. For the first time in as long as I could remember my stomach wasn't tied up in knots, and I was able to go more than five minutes without wondering what Martha was doing and if we would ever be able to get back together.

In the back of my mind was Larry's suggestion that I ask Mary to help me understand what is happening with Martha and the divorce.

Almost instantaneously my thoughts turned towards rejection. *What if she doesn't want to help? What if she sees it as weak? What if she hates all men right now?* The voices were strong. I was blindsided by Martha and her claims of unhappiness, and my confidence level was low. I wasn't looking for a relationship, but a rejection of any type would be devastating. I felt the anxiety set in. The beads of sweat on my forehead and the bouncing of my left leg were the first indications. Then my mouth was getting dry.

The room was extra loud at that moment. It was the perfect time. I was dealt another monster hand, two aces. I had to ask her right then or I never would. I folded the hand and turned to Mary.

"I am having a really hard time right now." I started in a very quiet voice. "I don't understand why this is happening with Martha and why she won't talk to me," I continued without hesitation. "Could we talk some time, and you can give me your perspective? We could go for a coffee or a drink and talk. Maybe you can help me understand."

There was a moment of silence. I was sure in my mind that she was questioning my sincerity. I hoped she would believe me. I needed some insight to move on. Maybe Larry was right, and she could provide it.

I was relieved to see a compassionate look on her face as she said, "Yes, I would love to talk with you about it."

I believed her sincerity. Maybe I could get some understanding. Mary grabbed my hand and squeezed it. I felt my body relax, maybe there was hope in me finding a way to find some relief.

A couple of hands later, Riley seemed to be bored and was getting restless. "It is getting late; Riley and I should go." Mary shared. "I have to show houses early in the morning."

Although I really didn't want her to go, I told her I understood.

"Let me walk you out." I suggested.

"No, play cards and good luck," she answered. It probably was for the best.

I stood up to hug her goodbye and thank her for the conversation. I assured her I would call soon. After shaking Riley's hand and telling him goodbye, I sat back down at the table. There were only twelve of us left playing. I hadn't noticed what was happening in the room over the last hour.

I watched Mary and Riley say their goodbyes and walk out. I had made a friend. At the time I had no idea what that meant, but it felt right. I had an empty feeling when she walked up the stairs and out of sight. Loss had been a big part of my life lately and I felt it again at a lesser level. I had felt that strange energetic attraction again. It was like I was meant to be around her.

I'd taken Larry's advice after all, and to my relief, I somehow knew she'd help me feel better—she already had, after just a couple of hours! I felt this was the beginning of a beautiful friendship.

I was conflicted in my thoughts. I felt the sadness of losing Martha come over me and the tears forming in my eyes. At the same time, I sensed a twinge of hope over the ache in my heart. I had to go before I broke down. I wanted hope and felt guilty for it. I couldn't face any goodbyes; I just stood up and left.

I couldn't help but feel the long walk through that beautiful house was a metaphor for the next few months. A journey through the magnificence of everything around me, feeling mostly alone and not knowing when it may end. But I had a new friend, and I knew in my deepest being I would be okay.

It was a few short weeks before we agreed to meet for dinner at Mary's favorite restaurant. It had the perfect vibe with an open kitchen and centralized bar. Everyone dining in the booths and at the high tops could be part of the excitement generated throughout the restaurant. She liked everything about it. Even the music was exactly as expected, just loud enough, and always the right beat to support any celebration.

The booth we were seated at was just in front of the expansive bar that glowed from all the candles reflecting their light on a mirrored backdrop. It was the perfect setting to get to know each other a little better.

The energy was high, but I was cautious because I wanted to share but I didn't know how much. There had to be a reason we were put together once again by Larry. There just had to be. I thought we both felt it. And I hoped we both wanted to know.

I began sharing with Mary that my divorce from Martha was a wake-up call which made me question what had been missing in my life. I shared that my life had hit rock bottom. As Mary looked over the rim of her wine glass, I could tell that in her heart, she knew it really wasn't a disaster at all. She knew something I didn't at that moment. She shared with me later in the night that I was in the "energy of possibility," and I was in the "vibration of love at its purest source." She shared that the love I was feeling and expressing had the potential of tremendous physical love but it was also much bigger. I marveled at her reassurance, but I wasn't convinced.

We didn't know then, but this was the beginning of a love story that was beyond either of our past experiences and was going to stretch our dreams of what was possible.

As I shared what I was learning and feeling, we drank wine, ate the best food, and didn't notice there was anyone else in the restaurant. Every plate delivery was in perfect timing and there was never a break in the flow of the energy or the conversation. I could tell by the look in Mary's eyes, we were having similar feelings. We were experiencing true love and true connection between us. It was the beginning of not only a love story, but *our* love story.

As I was sharing how I was questioning my life, what I had done wrong, and what was missing, she was hearing loud and clear that I was answering my heart's calling to acknowledge where I was right then and who I was with. I felt I was lost, and she knew I'd been found.

I wouldn't know until months later that Mary knew that night in an irrefutable way that she was staring at her twin flame and acknowledged herself for calling me in for a purpose greater than just two people enjoying life. She wondered if I had realized the same thing. She wondered if I was feeling the magic of two people having been called to find each other no matter what was right, in spite of society's rules, and despite our fears of rejection.

She knew we were creating our future, stepping into our purpose, and birthing hope, but I wasn't that awake. Yet.

Moment of Reflection

When we miss or choose not to pay attention to our promptings, they will come again. But what I have found is, they only come when the energy is aligned. Another way to say it would be that the promptings come when we are in the space and place to take action on them. In my case with Mary, the first prompting I missed because I wasn't in a position to act on it. The energy wasn't aligned again for ten years. The second prompting came, and I was ready to take action.

Promptings can come in many different ways, and they are different for all of us. It is essential that we learn our ways of receiving these valuable messages. And yes, we all get them. I believe that by paying attention when there is a strong feeling or a pull to do or *not* do something is a great place to start. Notice this feeling and where it shows up in the body (i.e., maybe the heart or stomach). It is common for people to experience a gut feeling, but that's not the only visceral reaction. Some people experience the feeling of the hair on the back of their necks standing up. Others have a ringing in their ears. Take the time to notice and be prepared to take action.

What about fear? We all experience it. Most, if not all of us are afraid of the unknown. It only makes sense, if we have never experienced something before, then we don't know how to deal with it. The promptings to move forward only show up in the best interest of a person. Remain open to the possibilities that come with the promptings. And if a prompting is ignored or missed, don't worry, it will come back when the timing is right, and the energy is aligned.

Chapter Eight
Too Spiritual for Me

*Beliefs can be the most empowering things as
you experience your creations and co-creations.
They also can be the cause of devastating
results. Wars have been fought, relationships
ended, and lives destroyed over them.*

The Round Table, channeled by Vince Kramer

W e all have a belief system that is our filter through which we look at life. This system consists of beliefs that we form throughout our lifetime. At birth, we already have some of our neural networks wired based on our parents and grandparents. From day one, we begin to form other beliefs that affect the way we see life and how we make our decisions which are the basis for the perceptions we have for the circumstances we experience.

The majority of our beliefs are formed by the time we are two years old and most of them are solidified by the time we are seven years old. They mostly come from two places. We either accept and take on beliefs of others or we develop our own from our perceptions of what happened around us.

As a young child before the brain is fully developed, it is basically a sponge. Individuals take on the beliefs of parents, grandparents, teachers, and other influential people in life. There are also basic needs that must be met. There is an innate drive to be safe, loved, and fed. When actions resulted in any of those needs being met, a belief around that action formed. When needs aren't met, there are also beliefs around those actions. Some of these beliefs empower us, but many of them limit us. In some ways, we see the world and make decisions based on the perceptions of a two-year-old.

The good news is that our beliefs aren't real. They are just something that we choose to accept, hold on to, and use to live our lives.

Our beliefs are challenged all the time. The question is: Are we going to continue looking at beliefs as right or wrong? Or is it time to look at them as empowering or disempowering?

Mary and I established a routine of getting together once a month to catch up and share our experiences of divorce and single life. I was really enjoying time out as friends. It had been about ten months since we started this scheduled time together and we were becoming good friends.

One night was especially nice. We chose Carlos' Bistro, a more upscale restaurant. It was an easy drive for both of us and just the right atmosphere for our seemingly deeper and deeper conversations.

As I got closer to the restaurant, I pictured the radiance of her smile. I had become accustomed to it and the way I felt when I was around her. I could see the glow of the neon sign above the restaurant.

We both ordered a beautiful glass of cabernet and settled into the body-hugging leather chairs at a very comfortable and cozy table off to the side. We were seated under a rather large neon light that shouted out the name of the restaurant and owner. Carlos is a very stylish Latin man with kind eyes and a caring demeanor. Mary looked extra attractive in the blue glow of the neon light. The other patrons didn't know we were just friends, so I'm sure I was the envy of many of the men seated around us.

The wine was exceptional. It was smooth with a hint of black pepper, and I enjoyed every sip. It didn't take long for us to get into another intriguing conversation after quickly catching up on each other's lives over the past three weeks. We had both been in transition, dating, adapting, surviving. It was nice to have someone to share the trials and tribulations of life with.

As we began to enjoy an expertly prepared and presented dinner, our conversation turned to religion, spirituality, and Mary's beliefs about life. After twelve years of Catholic school, I had some very ingrained beliefs, and I was challenged by many of the spiritual concepts she was presenting.

Between bites of her crusted salmon, she shared her thoughts on the Universe, energy, oneness, twin flames, and many terms I wasn't familiar with. Some were easy for me to grasp and accept. Others, not so much.

After we both had just taken a drink of our wine, Mary said, "You know, I went to Catholic school for a few years too." She continued sharing a concept I agreed with, but not necessarily in the same way she presented it. She stated with certainty, "We are all one and we are all a part of God, meaning: In a way we are God."

I wanted to blurt out, "Wait just a minute!" But instead, I said, "What do you mean 'we are all a part of God'?"

Mary smiled and continued, "I know this goes against what we have been taught, especially in Catholic school, but God wanted to know itself, so as energy it split itself into aspects to experience itself."

This time I did say politely, "Whoa wait a minute, why would God need to experience himself?"

Mary replied, "Well, I have no idea exactly how to answer you in a way that would satisfy your mind, but I can share my understanding." She put her fork down and focused all of her attention on me and began again, "My understanding is that God as energy split off or multiplied the energy so there could be innumerable aspects of this energy experiencing life."

I asked, "What do you mean it '*split off*'?"

She replied, "The energy first split in two and then those two halves split in two and so on until there were twelve strands. We know them as the twelve tribes from the Bible. In God wanting to experience itself, the end goal is for the energies to re-unite and become whole again."

I had to think about that statement. I am someone who needs to digest and contemplate new concepts. In my silence Mary went on, "Have you heard of twin flames?"

"No, I've never heard of twin flames, what do you mean by that?" I responded quizzically.

"Well, twin flame means, exact opposite." I nodded knowingly, but obviously encouraged her to continue by the look on my face. "Twin flame energy means that one energy is split into two energies, each energy having different aspects of the one energy." That I got, but Mary could see I still didn't completely understand.

"Let me give you an example," she offered, "My mom has a twin flame, actually a few but that is for another time. The one that is most relevant is a man she was with for just over a year. What is important about this example is that she never felt so complete, and she never felt so fulfilled than that year with him. Don't get me wrong, they had very challenging times together as a couple, but what was so fascinating was how she felt when she was with him. They completed each other and helped each other grow."

I liked what I was hearing, but I wanted to know what the purpose of a twin flame was.

"When twin flame energies find each other," Mary began, "the purpose is to come into union. Coming into union means understanding that the two energies or the two people are exact identical opposites of each other. When these two people do their work to be in harmony with one another even though they are showing each other their opposites, there is a merging of the energies back into the one energy. And that's the purpose for God splitting the energies, to come back into wholeness or oneness." She added, "There are now thousands or hundreds of thousands of these split-off energies looking for their twin flame to come back into wholeness."

I was intrigued and wanted to know who Mary thought her twin flame was, but wasn't sure I wanted to hear the answer, instead I asked her, "Can you share an example of a twin flame I might know?"

"Probably the best-known way for me to share is to use Jesus as an example. Jesus was born into a family or a tribe, one of the twelve tribes!"

I was torn between thinking this was all "way-out-there" talk and finding it all fascinating. I couldn't wait to hear more. I was experienced with keeping my composure and not exposing my thoughts by the look on my face. That's what I did. I wanted her to share more.

Just before I took another bite of my dinner, I encouraged her, "Tell me more."

She enthusiastically continued, "There is a lot more to the characters in the Bible such as his mother, father, and uncles etc. than you know. They had awareness of what I'm sharing with you, and they were on Earth to share many things. One of the most important is that we are energy and a part of God."

Mary took a sip of wine, smiled, and said, "Hold on for this one, but Mary Magdalene was the twin flame of Jesus. They are probably the most famous example of a twin flame relationship. They completed each other energetically. In truth, Mary Magdalene was way more powerful and important a figure than we have been told in the Bible. Jesus—actually his Hebrew name was Yeshua—and Mary Magdalene were to teach us and be the example of coming together in wholeness and union. Yeshua and Mary Magdalene were twin flames. They completed each other energetically."

"Fascinating," was my reply.

Several times through this and other exchanges, I caught myself cutting my beautifully prepared medium rare ribeye into tiny little pieces as a way of hiding. My beliefs were being threatened even though I didn't feel she was challenging me. It was a reaction very unlike me. Rarely have I hidden from a conversation.

We tend to believe that we know the truth, the only truth. Unfortunately, like so many others, I had learned what I believed was *the right way*. What others believed—if that didn't align with my beliefs—was wrong. I wasn't alone. When it comes down to it, that is the reason for all the strife and wars we have experienced.

I liked my time with Mary, so I chose not to outwardly question her beliefs. But often we feel if what someone else believes is right, that makes us wrong. This results in each party doing whatever it takes to be right because they don't want to be wrong. This is the basis for all the wars.

Our beliefs are who we are, what we stand for. Once we are ready to accept that if others' beliefs are right for them which doesn't make our beliefs any less right, or even wrong, then we can find a foundation to try and understand each other.

This wasn't the first time Mary had me squirming in my chair with her outlook on life. She was different from the other people I'd known. That's why I really liked her. She was intriguing and refreshing. But still I felt uncomfortable as she challenged twelve years of religious education and fifty years of living.

I liked this woman and I wanted to be open to the possibilities that she shared. At the same time, I was tired of religion and the dogma associated with it. I felt like I had a tug of war in my head, and I was frantically pulling on both ends. Some of what she said made sense and some seemed to be contradictory to all my beliefs. But I liked her, and I enjoyed the times I was able to spend with her. I felt heard and listened to, really understood, even in this uncomfortable conversation.

Carlos had been attentive throughout our entire time there, checking back with us from time to time to see if we needed anything. I appreciated the high-quality customer service but at the same time, I wished this elegant man with his tie thrown over his left shoulder would allow our conversation to go on uninterrupted.

Somewhere in the midst of my uneasiness, she shared that she has an energetic connection to the Holy Family. I accidentally knocked my spoon off the adequate but completely full table. I'm not sure if I was just clumsy or shocked by the comment. Never have I heard anyone suggest any type of connection to Jesus, Mary, or Joseph.

I was intrigued with everything that Mary had to say, but it pushed and challenged my beliefs. I was feeling uncomfortable. Finally, I said, "Some of this makes sense to me, even fills in some holes. But what does that have to do with now?"

I watched Mary take a few bites of food and sips of wine. I could tell she was contemplating what to share and what not to say. She settled into her chair getting comfortable, put her fork down and replied to my question.

"The lineage of Jesus, Mary Magdalene, Mary, and Joseph has been passed down through the years to continue sharing The Message," she answered, pausing only a second before continuing. "My mom has been told and I have been told that we are part of that lineage. I mean everyone is, but we are a soul family that carries the same energy and are here to help bring that same message again."

"What do you mean 'The Message'?" I asked believing I knew the answer but doubting myself in the context of this challenging but enlightening discussion.

Seemingly frustrated, Mary exclaimed, "In one phrase, it is Christ Consciousness. You might call it the Golden Rule. The message is, we are all one, we are on this Earth to love one another and take care of each other. It is about having compassion and real empathy. You know, what the Holy Family was all about."

Just then, my mind jumped back to what she was saying before I asked this question. I interrupted yet again, "So do you believe you are reincarnated? And if you do, from whom?"

"I believe there are many, many people that carry the energy of the Holy Family, yes. I believe that I carry the energy of Mother Mary and my mom carries the energy of the grandmother of Jesus," she stated with certainty.

Now this caught me by surprise, and I wasn't sure how to feel. All I know is I had to hear more, even though I thought this was a pretty bold claim! I urged her to go on.

"I know this sounds unbelievable, but I feel this." she said. "It's so bizarre how so many of my family members are here in the same place with the same awareness just like in those times."

This was a little more than I could handle, so I blurted out, "I think you are just too spiritual for me." Even though I had basically terminated the conversation with those words, I still searched her face for any indication of how she felt.

By the look on Mary's face and the cooler feeling at the table, I had a sinking feeling that my comment may have shut her down. What she shared was intriguing, still I didn't know if my beliefs were in alignment. I remembered the unmistakable connection I felt in Cabo San Lucas. I couldn't deny it, but it might not matter any longer. Maybe our chance was gone. She looked at me like she was thinking, *Ah ha, I knew it. I trusted him enough to share these "out there" things and sure enough he couldn't accept any of it.*

I hoped I was wrong because I wanted her to trust me.

I wasn't going to find out that night. As the conversation moved towards surface level chit chat, it was obvious the deeper conversation was over at least for this night. In fact, I think I may have stepped over the line. I could tell that she was disappointed in my response.

I understood the concept of one true energy that Mary called *the Universe* or *Source*. But I had been taught to believe in God as a trinity of beings that are superior to each and every one of us. Did she not believe in God? I had often questioned the overall concept, especially the way it was taught to me in grade school. But never had I considered the possibility of God in any other way than I was taught. Never had I considered the possibility that there is no heaven or hell. And I definitely had never considered the possibility of anyone I know being an energetic or a direct physical descendent of any member of the Holy Family. I realized that the concepts that she'd shared may be confusing because they were so foreign to me. I was willing to question my beliefs, but I felt we were talking more about a religion than a way of life. I wasn't interested in a new religion. That was just in my mind because of my internal definition of spirituality.

We continued light conversation over dessert as we shared a near-perfect flan. We both steered the conversation away from the sensitive topics that were obviously so dear and important to this deep and captivating woman. I was greatly relieved and at the same time extremely sad when it was time to go home. It was going to take me a while to consider what she had said. Yet, I still didn't want to leave her company. I was overloaded with these new concepts. They were beliefs obviously very important to her and so very foreign to me.

As I walked her to the car, I found myself searching for the courage to share my feelings despite the somewhat awkwardness of the last part of our evening. The tug of war was still happening in my head and my heart wanted to take control. We arrived at her sparkling-clean white Lexus waiting to take her away from me. I leaned up against the car as she unlocked the door. I was just looking at her, taking in her energy. The energetic attraction that I experienced the very first time I saw her hadn't gone away. I didn't understand that either. I knew there was a special connection between us, and I didn't want to ruin that by sharing either of the things that were going through my mind at this time. I somehow found the courage to temporarily move beyond those things that had been bouncing back and forth in my head like ping-pong balls.

I don't remember how I moved beyond the fear that she was too spiritual for me; I knew that proclamation may cost me a relationship with her. I quieted the voices in my head long enough to share my other confession, "I really like you a lot" as I leaned in, and we had our first kiss. And it was nice, I felt it all the way to my toes. Yet I worried about the spirituality comment. As we said our good nights, I secretly didn't want her to go.

Moment of Reflection

I know now that wanting to hold on to old beliefs "to be right" is what we do because if we question a belief or a set of beliefs, we may have to look at what resulted from those beliefs in the past. Where might we have been happier? Or more successful? Where did we turn away someone who could have been very important to us? Or missed an opportunity? We have all let things, people, and possibilities slip through our hands because of beliefs we clung to, not knowing that beliefs aren't real.

What I also understand in hindsight is the importance of being open to new ways, new beliefs. When we open our hearts and minds to listen to, see, and experience new ways without judgment, we give ourselves the opportunities to choose new ways, new beliefs, that empower us to grow and expand. We can choose to see the world in a new way, a way that supports us in discovering the unlimited possibilities of the Universe and our ability to create a new reality. We can't grow or expand holding tightly to the same beliefs, doing the same things, or thinking the same thoughts.

On the short drive home, I fought with the mixed emotions I was feeling. I really liked this woman. She was smart, kind, and different from most people I knew. And there still was that strange energy attraction that was pulling me towards her. There was something special between us and Mary's beliefs around spirituality and oneness explained it. But I didn't know if I could bring myself to question everything I built the first fifty years of my life around.

I knew that this was something special and the perfect reflection of something that we were feeling. But I also knew I shared that I had a problem with something that was extremely important to her, spirituality. I didn't know how right I was on the latter at that very moment. I wasn't ready to change my beliefs just to have a relationship in this moment. But I was willing to begin to question my beliefs.

After all, something had been missing my entire life. Maybe, my beliefs were the reason. The seed was planted, and I was ready to learn more.

Chapter Nine

The Ugly in The Mirror

*The biggest obstacles to a happy, fulfilled life
come from within. You must uncover them, learn
why they were developed, and move beyond
them. There is a gift in each of them. When you
find the gift, you will no longer be challenged by
them.*

The Round Table, channeled by Vince Kramer

One of the most important things I realized during my journey
that is documented in this book, is that we are all energy. To
best understand and live the life we are meant to live, it is essential
for us to learn just what that means. When we become familiar with
the concepts of quantum physics and the universal laws of energy,
we can make the most of life's experiences in becoming all that we
are meant to be and accomplishing all that we are meant to do.

The most known and helpful of the universal laws is the law of
attraction. Basically, the law of attraction states that like attracts
like. In the book *The Secret*, we learn that we can implement the
law of attraction to manifest what we want into our lives. But the

law of attraction can also help us see and understand ourselves better.

Because we are energy, we send a vibration out into the Universe. This vibration has a certain frequency. Through the law of attraction, we attract people with a "like vibration" into our lives. These people truly show us ourselves. The concept is known as mirroring where we see ourselves in the people we attract. When we see things we like and when we see things we don't like in others, both are a reflection of who *we* are and the energy we are putting out.

The emotions that we experience during the interactions are mirrors for us to see ourselves. These mirrors are showing us where there is work to be done in learning to love each and every part of ourselves. We create the interactions and circumstances so we can learn and grow. Some circumstances are pleasant while others are challenging, yet looking for—and finding—the gift in all of them will benefit us greatly.

Mary and I had been friends and happy-hour buddies for many months. During that time, we could never seem to be in the same place to be able to try and take our relationship to the next level. When the opportunity finally showed up, I asked her to join me on a long layover in Anchorage. We had an amazing time taking advantage of the midnight sun. Our first real date was a huge success that I jeopardized on the way home.

As a black Chevrolet Camaro with heavily tinted windows darted in front of me with barely enough room between the car in the right lane and my full-size Ford Pickup in the passing lane, I lost it. I mean, I really lost it. I blurted out at the top of my voice, "You stupid son of a b$%#h, you are a self-centered a$$hole," as I pressed down hard on the gas pedal to catch up to this inconsiderate driver. Although I moved into fight or flight mode almost immediately, I finally remembered where I was and who I was with on this early morning drive home, and I stopped the pursuit.

Immediately, I was bouncing from emotion to emotion just like the ball in a highly active pinball game. Anger, frustration, guilt, and shame were all there. Almost all at the same time. Embarrassed by my volcanic outburst, I looked over at Mary. She stared straight ahead, squeezing the handle of the door. My grip on the steering wheel was even tighter than before and I stared at the car in front of me as if I were piercing it with some type of destructive rays. My anger wasn't about that driver any longer, it was all turned towards myself. I couldn't say a word. Mostly because I didn't know what to say; my rant was unacceptable, especially in front of Mary.

Why do I act like this? What is my problem?

I have the answers now, but I certainly didn't understand at the time. When we are born, we start to form a personality or an ego that will be our operating system for life. Our life situations and the people in our life help us develop this main personality. That is why we chose our parents and where we were born. Everything came together perfectly in our choices to develop this personality to live the life we are meant to live.

But things happened during our life where we didn't feel safe and didn't know how to deal with the problem through our main personality. When this happened, we developed sub-personalities, or other ego personalities, to deal with the problem. These sub-personalities are always with us and when similar circumstances happen in our day-to-day lives, these sub-personalities are triggered and strike out to protect us. If we don't become aware of these personalities and what triggered them, we have no control of when they appear and what we will do under their influence. The reactions tied to these personalities can be devastating as they try to protect us at any cost. This can affect our relationships and every other part of our lives.

This was only the third time we had been in a vehicle together. The other two I didn't experience a driver that I thought was inconveniencing me or being dangerous. All I could think about was, *This might be our last.* The silence between us was deafening. Everything I thought to say seemed inadequate at best and a lame excuse at its worst.

And then, Mary broke the silence, "Where is that driver showing you a part of yourself?"

We were about to enter an explosive minefield made up of our individual beliefs, life experiences, and past relationships. These beliefs, relationships, and experiences are different for each of us, and because they are different in many ways, we look at life differently. Each of us has our truth and it is different from the other's. I was yet to learn that we can have different truths and it doesn't make the other wrong.

At that very moment Mary asked me about the driver, a bomb went off in the truck, actually it went off inside of me. I'm not sure how I just didn't explode all over everything. I internally screamed: *f@#$.* Luckily it was in my head and never left my mouth. As I continued to have thoughts like *Who does she think she is? Where does she get off judging me?* I searched for something to say that wouldn't destroy the two days that we just had together like an out-of-control wrecking ball can destroy the foundation of a building.

Instead, I stayed silent.

Once again Mary was the one to break the silence, "I can tell you think I'm judging you. Maybe I am, but what is most important to me is, we just spent all of yesterday talking about this. We talked about shadows and people mirroring back to us what we are or can't be with."

It was true we talked about it, but at that very moment I could not see how it applied. I knew exactly what she was referencing consciously. Less than a week ago she gave me a Debbie Ford CD that talked about our shadows. But I wasn't connecting ego with shadow. I wasn't aware enough to make the connection. Shadows are those parts of ourselves that others show us in their actions.

Those things about ourselves that we won't let ourselves be or that we hide about ourselves from others. The CD made sense, but what did that have to do with this situation? What did it have to do with me? I hadn't done the work that Mary had. I hadn't learned these concepts. And to be honest at that very moment, I didn't think I needed to do any shadow work. I know now I was wrong and what happened next was a big clue.

I had many mixed emotions as Mary continued, "I want to help you see this, but you may need more time to think about it. Transformation takes a lot of acceptance. It takes a lot of uncovering all the parts of you that simply need to be healed. These parts of you are aspects of ego."

As Mary innocently shared, it was my ego that reacted that way; my blood pressure and adrenaline both shot right out of the open sunroof. My grip on the steering wheel was even tighter than when that Camaro, driven by the person that started this, sped around me. My body was tense and ready to defend itself from this perceived attack. *What? What? What are you talking about?*

I'm not sure if I actually said it or the words were just violently echoing in my head. Being completely unaware of what our ego actually was at that point in my life, I believed she was calling me egotistical or arrogant. These were the very things that I worked so hard not to be. And then, someone I thought was my friend and believed there was a future with, was calling me these heart-piercing words. It was more than I could take. I kept pushing her to explain; asking—no, demanding—she tell me why she thought I was egotistical. The short exchange was just a blur; I didn't hear anything over the voices in my head.

"I am not egotistical," I retorted, not really understanding what she meant. I didn't understand that our ego and alter egos are the same things as our personality and sub-personalities. I wasn't egotistical and feeling like Mary was insinuating I was, got another one of those ego personalities worked up. "Why do you think I have an ego?" I kept on.

I don't remember much of the conversation from that point forward because I was overcome by those two sub-personalities. They don't show up very often, but I know them. One of them wants to protect me from people who are trying to hurt me, and another wants me to be liked at any cost. When they show up together, their interests are always competing against each other, causing a chorus of fighting voices in my head.

As Mary said less and less, I had to do something.

"I'm sorry," I finally admitted. "I guess I'm just tired from flying all night."

Then it happened, she just stopped talking all together. When I pushed her harder to explain to me what she meant and why she felt that way about me, she said nothing. I was wanting answers. And I did what we all do, I made-up reasons in my head why she would do that to me, our relationship, and to her. All I could think of was that she didn't get me, she doesn't really see me, and it's obvious by her shutting down that she might not be interested in ever seeing me again. I am a good person, but I certainly wasn't showing it. And I wanted a chance to prove I wasn't egotistical or a bad guy. I was restless as I squirmed around on the cloth seats, adjusting the unusually restrictive seatbelt.

When our conversation did resume, it turned to casual but sporadic acknowledgments of the weather, other cars, or the scenery. It was nothing like the talks we had just days before. The remaining hour of the drive was awkward and discouraging. It was just as uncomfortable for Mary. I could hear the frustration in her voice.

I pushed her one more time as I began to feel not just a possible serious relationship, but our entire friendship, was in jeopardy, "If this is going to work, you have to talk to me. Tell me why you think I have an ego, why you feel I think I'm better than other people?

"Vince, I'm sorry I have nothing more to say," she said reluctantly. "I feel like I've tried to explain this concept to you. You probably think I'm judging you. I can't help that you are feeling that way. But I've lived most of my adult years with someone who had outbursts like you just had and then thought the outbursts were acceptable, just a way of letting off steam, never considering the people left in the wake of those outbursts. When you are the one in the wake, you learn to stop talking and not feel—to shut down. And changing the conversation to the weather or other non-triggering things becomes a way of life."

I moved to new emotions, guilt and shame. And I shut down.

When I finally maneuvered the truck the final few yards to her house, I felt panic wash over me. *What am I going to say? How is this going to end? Is it the end?*

I pulled into the driveway and slowly put the truck in park. Everything seemed like slow motion as I turned off the key, unbuckled my seat belt, and opened the door of the truck. I couldn't delay any longer. As I pulled her luggage gingerly out of the bed of the truck. I wondered if I would ever see it again, would I ever see *her* again. It was awkward for both of us as we said goodbye. I muttered something stupid like, "I've got to get home and change clothes" and "see you later." As we hugged, I couldn't help but want to hold on. This wasn't how I expected or wanted this trip together to end. I never wanted it to end.

Moment of Reflection

Without having done extensive personal work with someone who understands the parts of ourselves that we hide, a person might not understand what happened there. I know I didn't at the time. We haven't been taught about our belief system, ego personalities, and the shadows we hide from ourselves and others. On this two-hour-drive from the Denver International Airport to Mary's home, I experienced all three in a very disturbing way. We all have these parts of ourselves that we don't really know what to do with, so we bury them or try to hide them from ourselves and others.

They are all like beach balls that we are trying to keep hidden under the surface of the water. We try to keep them out of sight. But then something happens that diverts our attention and one of those balls pops above the surface. We divert our attention to that ball and another one shoots up into plain sight. What we thought we could keep hidden sabotages us.

We have to learn to embrace and love every part of ourselves before we can do what it takes to choose more empowering ways to create our reality. It is not about hiding or denying those parts of ourselves. Science tells us there are no mistakes or coincidences in life. Everything has its place and its purpose.

Experiences like this give us the opportunity to learn more about ourselves, to grow and expand into the powerful creators that we are meant to be.

Chapter Ten
What Have I Done?

Notice your emotions and the condition of your body. They are messengers that show you where the vibration of your energy is in that moment. Each showing you in its own way if you are in or out of alignment with the real you and what you have already created.

The Round Table, channeled by Vince Kramer

Promptings or messages show up in our lives in many ways. Some of the easiest messages for us to interpret are the ones we get from our emotions and body.

We are energy and as energy we have a vibration. This vibration can vary based on who and what we are at any given moment. When our thoughts and actions are positive and in alignment with who we truly are, we are at a high vibration. When our thoughts and actions are more negative and not supporting us, we emanate a lower vibration.

Our emotions are truly a communication system that helps us understand where our vibration is at that point in time. Emotions also have a vibrational frequency that range from the lowest vibration of fear and despair, up to the highest vibration of love and joy. Our emotions show us where we are vibrationally in any given moment in comparison to our highest vibration.

When we are in the lower vibrations our body is affected also and can manifest as pain, illness, and other diseases even as severe as cancer. Our body, like our emotions, is showing us that we are out of alignment. It isn't saying that we've done something wrong or that we're bad people. When we don't allow ourselves to experience the lower vibrational emotions and we stuff them inside of us, the body will also take on the lower vibration and give us signs through pain and illness.

My guilt and shame from my drive with Mary was evident in the signs my body shared in the days following the episode.

For the second time that day, I felt an explosion building inside of me, but it wasn't anger like earlier. I tossed my bags off to the side as I flew through the garage door into my house. I wasn't worried about the new wood floors or anything else for that matter. As I slammed the door shut behind me because I needed to get in the door that it was blocking, I ripped my tie off and navigated around the clothes baskets I left on the floor of the mud/laundry room. I got past the obstacle course just in time to fling the toilet seat up and spewed vomit in the general direction of the toilet. Luckily, most of it made it into the awaiting bowl. Unfortunately, some didn't. But I didn't care. *Where did that come from and why?* As I began to stand up and survey the damage, the second wave came on just as fiercely as the first.

Just like a fierce Colorado storm, there was a crack of thunder inside me, and I showered the toilet again with vomit. This time it didn't seem to stop. It felt like an hour even though I knew it was only a few minutes. With tears running down my face, I sat there in terror and pain.

What was wrong with me today?

First, my pathetic performance on the drive home and then this. As voices in my head started to beat me up, I felt the possibility of yet another wave. My stomach felt like it was the agitator in the washing machine I was using to hold myself upright. I glanced at the truth-telling mirror positioned over the laundry sink. I was met by bloodshot eyes and sweat rolling down my face along with the tears from the strain I just experienced. I was sick, maybe sicker than I had been in the last ten years.

Worried it was going to happen again, I secured a purple towel out of the closest laundry basket and quickly wiped up as much as I could without triggering yet another volcanic eruption. I had to lie down, and I had to do it right then. But first, I needed something to catch any vomit from future episodes. The last thing I remembered was ensuring my empty trash can was within arm's reach in case I vomited again, then I curled up in the fetal position with my blanket protecting me. I was still shivering from the chills as I fell asleep.

I wasn't sure how long I was asleep, but I knew it had been well over twelve hours because it was pitch black outside. All I could see as I lifted my head high enough to see over the arm of the couch was the lights of the city shimmering at the bottom of the mountain. I squinted through my strain-caused bloodshot eyes to see the clock on the microwave that was at least thirty feet away. I couldn't read it, but it didn't matter. I didn't care. I literally pulled myself up into the sitting position. I was so weak. I used the arm of the couch to push myself up onto my feet and waddled across the open floor plan. First to the chair and then to the island and finally to the sink, I made my way to the distressed oak cupboard to get a glass for some water. I was completely out of fluids. I survived the seemingly impossible task and made it back to the couch before I collapsed into a shivering ball of human once again. I should have called someone, but who would I call? I didn't want to bother my friends. There was nothing that they could do.

Actually, I wanted to call Mary, but I couldn't bring myself to bother her after how I acted on the drive from the airport. She hadn't called or texted me. "She doesn't want to see you," I told myself as I gave into pain and fell back to sleep.

The next time I opened my eyes, the sun was beating on me through the twenty-foot-tall windows overlooking the city of Colorado Springs below. I was miserable, I felt like I did after an extremely physical football game... beat up! My stomach was still churning, my head beat like a bass drum, and my legs weak like a newborn colt. I was a mess. I was hoping this was a twenty-four-hour flu. But it had been that long since I made it to this overstuffed refuge the first time. I managed to wobble back to the bathroom. I felt no better than I did the day before. The next seemingly impossible task was back to the kitchen for another glass of water. I had the awareness to grab a package of saltine crackers as I stumbled back to the couch and another sixteen hours of illness-induced slumber.

The next time I opened my eyes, I still wasn't feeling human. It was dark again. As I just lay there staring at the city lights below, I tried to make sense of the last two days. There was no sense to be made. It had been thirty-six hours, a day and half. I still felt like someone had hit me in the head with one of my aluminum softball bats, and I swallowed the stand-up mixer that was still on the knead setting swirling around in my stomach. I did manage to eat most of the package of saltine crackers I'd grabbed earlier. I checked my phone to see if anyone may have called me. The battery was dead. I didn't care to find a charging cord. After turning on the TV, I fell asleep to comforting reruns of *Mayberry R.F.D.*

My body was definitely showing me that I was out of alignment. The guilt, shame, and anger I was feeling resulted in thoughts that didn't support me or my relationship with Mary. I was creating something in my mind that was taking me away from a relationship that we were both meant to have. As I experienced these lower vibrational frequencies, my body began to resonate with them and resulted in my being violently ill. The low vibration was manifest in being sick.

I slowly recovered over the next thirty-six hours. It was a full three days, seventy-two hours from getting home, before I took a shower and got dressed. I charged my phone and was devastated to learn that no one had called me or tried to contact me in any way for three days. But the most disturbing thing for me, there was nothing from Mary. What had I done? First the rage and anger in the truck and now no contact for three days. I wondered if she was concerned she didn't hear from me or perhaps she didn't care. I refrained from allowing myself to get angry about any of it or pummel myself with judgments again. It took me hours to get up the courage and practice the words enough to even have a little confidence to call her.

As the phone was ringing, I couldn't help but wonder what to expect. I called her cell phone. I hoped she would answer. When I heard the normal *hello* as she answered the phone, I felt relief course through my body.

"I wasn't sure I was going to hear from you, and I'm happy you called," she said.

"I've been deathly sick the last three days," I shared. "My cell phone battery completely lost its charge. I couldn't get off the couch long enough to find my charger."

"What! Wow! I just thought that our 'mirror' conversation on the way home from Alaska was the end for me... for us." she admitted. "I am always hesitant to share my beliefs because I have lost new friends this way. But I thought because we had spent the entire day walking around Alaska together talking about this very thing that I was safe pointing it out to you, the mirror." She shared almost acceptingly. "I was convinced we were done! But you were just sick!" I detected in her voice that she was relieved. There was a touch of humor.

Through the conversation, I learned she thought I was avoiding her just like I thought she was doing to me. In fact, she thought that I was giving up on her. It is amazing what our minds will do to us. We both believed that the other was going to leave the possibility of us. Our conversation went well, but there was something different, there was a distance—something I couldn't define. After the drive home from Alaska, I was worried about the end of all our possibilities.

This distance between us was minor compared to my fears.

Over the next two weeks, we talked regularly. The conversations became warmer and warmer. We were closing the distance that had developed. Although we weren't completely back to where we were before that dreadful drive home, I was seeing the possibilities again.

One advantage of being an airline pilot is having long layovers in amazing cities. I had one coming up in Washington, DC, and I thought it would be a great opportunity for Mary to satisfy her traveling bug and for the two of us to have some more quality time together, a great opportunity for a second date! When I asked her if she was interested, she said yes before I got all of the words out of my mouth.

We had over twenty-four hours in DC, and I was extremely excited to share a grand city that meant so much to me with someone who had never been there before. We explored the WWI and WWII Memorials, taking the time to read some of the names and looking for family members. We strolled around the Lincoln Memorial Reflecting Pool admiring the beauty of the national treasures and the nature surrounding them. We held hands as we walked around the Washington Monument and stood at the top of the stairs of the Lincoln Memorial. As we walked by or around each of the monuments, I could feel Mary moving deeper into her thoughts or maybe it was her memories. Strolling the length of the Vietnam Memorial, she was completely silent and obviously distracted. She didn't seem happy or maybe she was wishing she was someplace else.

There was a bench about 100 feet from the Vietnam Memorial and I thought it might be the perfect place to rest and maybe she would share with me what she was thinking.

"Would you like to sit down for a while and take in the sights?" I asked hoping her answer would be yes. Without answering, she moved towards the slatted wooden bench.

As we took a seat I asked, "Why so quiet? What are you thinking about?"

Mary shared, "I was thinking about my ex-husband, not him specifically but who he was."

I didn't feel like she missed him, but I could still feel the change in her mood and wanted to know more. What was causing this change in her? She was with me in DC, and we were having a great time. Was she holding back or was she still shut down from our drive weeks ago?

I inquired further with some hesitance, "What about him?"

It was about a minute before she responded, "Honestly, it is about you as much as it is him. I admire that you both served your country. As we explored these memorials, I was thinking about what that means."

Before I had a chance to say anything, she continued, "You both have dedication, discipline, and look at things in very similar ways. You both were military pilots. I'm sure you know Russ flew fixed-wing and helicopters. He served two tours in Vietnam." With a little pause she continued, "As a matter of fact, when I first started dating Russ it was right before the dedication to the Vietnam Memorial. He flew from San Francisco to meet up with his closest friend from Atlanta to witness the dedication. In a way, being near the monument has forced me to look at the similarities."

I listened intently as I could feel her pride and honor for those that served. She continued, "I wasn't raised around the military, so I had a lot of catching up to do in my marriage with Russ as an officer's wife. Despite our age difference I always felt welcomed by the other wives. I loved the community and was saddened when Russ retired a year after we were married."

As we continued to talk about what she had been thinking about and how I was similar to her ex-husband in many ways, I wondered if she was considering the similarities a bad thing. I just didn't know exactly how to broach the subject with her, so I boldly stated, "Maybe I am just the kind of guy you like!" and held my breath waiting for her to respond.

Unexpectedly, the strangest thing happened! Her mood changed almost instantaneously. I let out my breath with a sigh of relief. I knew I was taking a chance making such a statement.

The biggest smile came across her face. The same smile that has warmed my heart from the moment I met her. And she said with surprising certainty, "Well, yes I do."

I hoped she would go on because I wasn't sure how to ask her what had caused her mood change during our walk. Fortunately, she started talking.

"I have to be honest with you, Vince. Although I like men like you, I promised myself I wouldn't have another marriage where I couldn't be all of me." She continued without hesitation, "I had to live a separate life with Russ. I lived a life of separation. I hid my spirituality because his non-belief was stronger than his love for me. I can't live the rest of my life like that, and I won't."

As she stopped talking, she looked directly into my eyes. I knew a lot about her and her marriage, but this was shared with such intensity that I knew that whatever I shared next was going to be critical to any future I had with her.

I looked back at her with all sincerity and touched her hand. "Mary, I am really touched by what you have shared, and I can see how important this is to you. I appreciate your honesty. I don't know exactly what all this means yet, what *we* mean, but I need to know this…"

Mary quickly jumped in and reassured me, "I like you a lot and I am willing to take our relationship step by step as we learn from each other and get to know each other more." She had a look of hope in her eyes, and I had a deep feeling of hope in my heart.

After taking in what she said I continued, "I need you to know that I will never want you to be anything other than who you are."

As she often did, she jumped up and took my hand, and we headed towards dinner. Her mood had changed; our relationship had changed. I was feeling excited again as we enjoyed our last few hours before the end of my layover.

Chapter Eleven

Looking for Proof

You must open your mind to the unlimited possibilities in the Universe. There is no right or wrong, there just is. That awareness and understanding will set you free.

The Round Table, channeled by Vince Kramer

S tarting back as far as the mid-17th century, there has been a split or at least a division between science and religion. When Galileo stated that the Earth revolved around the sun, he faced a Roman inquisition. The split began. There are many theories on why the split grew wider and wider. It really doesn't matter for our purposes, just knowing there was and still is one is enough, though it is narrowing.

With the discovery of quantum mechanics and quantum physics, we began to see what the two sides believed. When science started looking at everything as energy and discovering how these energies work and interact with one another, many of the concepts of religion—more correctly *spirituality*—were seen in science. The principles of the sciences of energy in many ways reflected the universal laws. We learned a very valuable lesson: They aren't mutually exclusive.

I didn't learn quantum principles in school. I didn't learn them in any of my college courses. And I definitely didn't learn them in high school. In fact, these concepts aren't taught outside of higher-level college courses. It is a shame because they would help us to understand why and how things happen *for* us and *around* us. It would help us see what has seemed to be missing in our lives. Because I wasn't taught the concepts, I wasn't willing to see anything in a different way.

We all need to be willing to open ourselves to seeing and understanding things differently and then allow ourselves to be challenged by looking at something in a new way. We need a motivating force or reason to open ourselves to becoming aware of new ways to look at and, more importantly, see the world around us. We need a catalyst to encourage us to see our world in a new way, a more empowering way. Mary was that catalyst for me.

In Mary's first marriage, her husband wasn't interested in her thoughts or beliefs around life and spirituality, and she wasn't going down that road again. I knew she wanted to make sure I wasn't going to be like that. We had many conversations around our beliefs, and I remember one night in particular. It was unusually cool that evening and the green tint to the churning clouds above us signaled a fierce storm was about to take our conversation inside. It was just Mary and me sitting on her deck sharing about the challenges of our day. We were both still getting to know each other, and we loved each other's company.

With the crack of thunder in the distance, I made a comment about God and the angels bowling in heaven. Magically, the conversation turned to all the things in the past that directly led to the two of us sitting here and drinking a lovely glass of red wine together.

As Mary shared the events from the last fifteen years that led to her health scare and ultimate divorce, she used words like *attract* and *created*. I found it interesting that these were the words she used to describe situations in her life that were unpleasant and even horrifying, especially around the actions of others. It seemed to me that she had been taught to take responsibility for all the bad things that had happened in her life. Bad things happen. Why should she be responsible?

I wasn't there to psychoanalyze or debate why she used these words or chose to take responsibility. We were in the discovery phase of this new relationship. We were getting to know one another and conversations like this one were accelerating the process.

I wasn't sure if it was the impending storm or just knowing that my turn was coming to talk, but I was beginning to feel the hairs on the back of my neck standing up. I didn't necessarily agree, but I was not sure she wanted to know that I didn't. I couldn't stop fidgeting, either playing with my empty glass or folding and unfolding the napkin. Just as I started to share my thoughts and stories, the clouds opened up and the rain forced us inside.

We decided to go to Mary's bedroom where we could have some privacy and continue our conversation without interruption. She was the head of a household and sole provider for a full house. Besides Riley, her mom and adopted brother also lived with her. Riley was quite spirited and demanding of his mom's attention. He was also a teenager with disruptive mood swings. Joyce, her mother, also liked Mary's attention which created conflict between the two of them from time to time. I guess you could say hiding away in the bedroom was the quietest and most perfect option for us.

It was a great escape. She had a sitting area with two chairs and a small table overlooking a deck. We could see the lightning flashes and the sheets of rain caused by the strong and sometimes violent winds of the storm.

Tucked safely inside, it was my turn to share. I filled our wine glasses, leaned back on the comfortable chair, and crossed my legs. I swirled the wine in the glass for a minute or two before taking a long, deliberate sip. What was I waiting for, why was it so hard to start? Was the delay because it really didn't matter? Or maybe it was not accepting my fate? I am easy going and it felt like sharing was not accepting what had been put in front of me or judging her.

I started by saying that I wasn't sure why things had happened the way they had and that as I looked back at the last eight to ten years of life much of it didn't make sense to me. I told her that I was taught that God had a plan for us, and we don't ask questions. I know now it was a very predetermined view of life. Basically, I believed that I (we) have very little say in how our lives turn out, yet I was also taught that we have free will. The two sometimes seemed mutually exclusive. I went on to say that I didn't necessarily know what the plan for me was.

Our conversation immediately shifted gears as Mary asked me what I meant. I spent the next ninety minutes laying out for her my beliefs about God. I shared that I believed there was a plan for us, and He had a reason for what he puts in our life. I shared that the choice really wasn't up to me.

I could see she was curious as she asked me how that all works. I tried my best to explain a subject and a belief I was taught and held on to as I grew up without questioning. As our conversation continued, I got confused about what I learned in catechism and what my parents taught me. She wasn't making me wrong, but I knew by the doubtful look on her face, she didn't think I was right. When she asked me if I believed that I have no control over my life, I countered with free will. Then she challenged me with "Yet, you believe that God put a situation in front of you with specific results and you had no control." *Do I answer NO or YES?* Both are true. My answer to her was a question.

"What do you believe?"

"Well, I don't believe that we are given bad situations, so we learn a lesson or are driven in a certain direction," she states with great confidence. "I believe we experience circumstances in our lives that we create or that we co-create with others. We are responsible for the circumstances in our life. Yes, there are things to learn from them, but there is a gift in each of them."

Challenged again! She had once again made me look at a belief ingrained since childhood that I never questioned, just took on as one of my own, and that I never really thought about let alone wondered if it was true. The conversation continued for many more minutes, but my mind was locked into this old belief challenge. She didn't do it on purpose, but then I wanted to prove myself right.

On the drive to work the next day, our conversation was the only thing on my mind. I couldn't wait until lunch so I could do some research. I wanted to prove to myself I was right and then prove it to her. Mary had shared several things that have driven me to question my beliefs. And I wanted to defend my beliefs. I wanted to be right. So far, she had proven to have valid ideas about the different aspects of life. She hadn't proven that they were more right or more valid than mine. On the contrary, there were many I had questioned and found scientifically that she was right and then chose to question my own beliefs. I was sure this one would be different though.

As soon as I arrived at work, I learned that there was a training issue, and I was off to the races. No time to research. But the question and doubt weighed heavily on me.

Before I knew it, I was five hours into my day, so I slipped into the cafeteria to grab a sandwich. The room was packed, not an empty chair and I knew I wouldn't get any research done in the cafeteria. The training center was always busy. It operates three hundred sixty-three days a year and twenty-four hours a day. There are thirteen thousand pilots at United Airlines and coming to training is just as much about catching up on old friendships as it is about completing the annual training. As expected, there were groups of pilots spread throughout the spacious dining room with no available tables. It was quite loud. There was no way I'd get any quiet time there. I stealthily slid out before anyone noticed I was there.

I stepped back into my office quietly, turned off the light and pulled out my personal computer. It was time for some research. I was about twenty-five minutes into my lunch break when I got engrossed in quantum physics and the double-slit experiment. There were many new concepts to consider. The biggest was the observer effect and how the double-slit experiment proved it. The observer effect says the mere observation of a phenomenon inevitably changes the phenomenon. Basically, by observing the circumstances in our lives, we create our own reality through our perceptions. We create our life experiences. Once again, Mary's spiritual beliefs were proven right by science. I was coming to believe there is little if any separation between the two. Spirituality and science were saying the same thing and there was little separation between them.

Later that evening, I got my second dose of this new reality. I was looking through my Facebook page, the very first post was about a movie Mary recommended to me a few months back. My new word for all of these things showing up in my life was *synchronicity*. Mary was going to be busy that night and I made a date with my TV and DVD player to watch *What the Bleep Do We Know!?*

The movie was about quantum physics and consciousness. It is a combination of movie narrative, documentary-style interviews, and computer-animated graphics. I was mesmerized for the next one hour and forty-five minutes. I learned more about the observer effect. I began to understand at a deeper level the concepts of energy and the law of attraction. I saw the connection between science and spirituality right in front of my eyes. There was no denying it. I understood fully what Mary was sharing with me, and it all made sense. The interviews in the movie not only enlightened me, but also gave me plenty of people to research and books to read.

They introduced me to Dean Radin, senior scientist at the Institute of Noetic Sciences which was cofounded by astronaut Edgar Mitchell and Dr. Fred Alan Wolf, an independent quantum physicist and the author of the book *Taking a Quantum Leap*. I also learned about neuroscientist Candace Pert and her book, *Molecules of Emotion*. Another person of interest was Dr. Joe Dispenza, the author of *Evolve Your Brain: The Science of Changing Your Mind*. (Dr. Joe would later become one of my mentors.) A new world was opened up to me and for me. One of the concepts I learned from my study of quantum physics is there are no mistakes or coincidences. For years to come, I would see the importance of this movie in every aspect of life.

I couldn't wait to share this with Mary. I didn't know what it all meant, but I was ready for it all to make sense.

Moment of Reflection

It is very interesting to me how many things we take at face value. We accept what we have been told without questioning. If it is in a book or on the news, it is unquestionably true. We have been raised to respect our elders and believe the experts. We have been conditioned to believe if we have seen it on TV or the internet, it is real. It is beyond reproach. I've experienced it in what I thought possible or acceptable. Staying within the lines had kept me from following the knowingness of that little five-year-old. My eyes had been opened and my heart activated to lead the way. No more looking for the next job or title, it was time to create my life from the inside out.

When we accept a belief, opinion, or judgment and make it our own, it limits us from expanding our awareness and restricts us from seeing another way, even if it for our best good.

Chapter Twelve

An Unexpected Surprise

Pay attention to what happens in your life. Your creations are assisting you in living on purpose, Your Unique Purpose.

The Round Table, channeled by Vince Kramer

One of the hardest concepts from quantum physics is that there are no mistakes or coincidences in our lives. What that means is there truly is a reason for everything that happens in our lives. In fact, we are responsible for creating or co-creating all our circumstances. In my childhood, I heard all the time growing up that everything happens for a reason. That was very hard to accept especially when things happened to me that I saw as bad.

But that is how I saw it from the perspective of a child. A perception formed before the reasoning part of my brain even started to develop. The reasoning part of the brain is the frontal lobe, and it doesn't start to develop for use until we are seven. It usually finishes developing in our late twenties. Now, as I looked back at these circumstances with an adult mind, a reasoning mind, I am able to see the creation of and the gift in every one of those events. Even though I learned that I created something and learned that there was a gift in it didn't mean I was willing to allow it or accept it. We develop beliefs on the circumstances of the past that we aren't so willing to give up.

When we attract others into our lives, they are often messengers for what we need to know or learn. Most of the time they show us with their energy or their actions. Sometimes, they receive a message to be shared with us. It may be one that is consciously shared or maybe shared unconsciously without them even realizing.

We truly get in our own way. Our belief systems and sub-personalities sabotage us. We might believe we don't deserve something, or we believe we aren't smart enough, thin enough, or attractive enough. Other times, because we can't see the "how," we don't even want to try. Our beliefs keep us in a very small box. A box that doesn't let us see the possibilities.

Another way our beliefs can completely stop us in our tracks is when we refuse to question them, and we stay stuck in the same old rut. There was a ten-year period before the divorce, where I was stuck in a rut and going nowhere. I promised myself at the Canfield workshop that I would try everything once and decide if it would work for me or not. I knew I had to have an open mind if I was going to show up in the world authentically. I'm so glad that I made that decision because what Mary was going to share with me would push me in ways I had never been pushed before.

And would change my life forever.

One event that stands out in my mind is some time I shared with Mary just before leaving on a five-day retreat to Vancouver, British Columbia. I had just arrived home from work and was climbing around my storage closet trying to find the retreat information. I couldn't remember exactly what I was supposed to take to the intensive, so I had to find the information before I packed. Suddenly, the phone began to ring. I rushed downstairs just in time to catch the call before it went to voicemail.

I answered the ringing phone my typical way, "Vince Kramer."

"Hi," I heard Mary say on the other end of the line with a little bit of fun in her voice.

It was good to hear from her and I told her so. I hadn't talked to her for a few days and this event I was going to was going to cause me to be "radio silent" for the entire five-day retreat.

"What are you doing?" she asked.

"Buried in a heap of papers in one of my closets looking for some information for this retreat I'm going to this weekend," I shared with her.

Mary excitedly explained that she was up in Aspen with her son and business partner and asked if I'd like to join them.

"Oh, I don't know," I finally said after her insisting several times. "I have an early flight to Vancouver in the morning."

Mary teasingly said, "You don't know what you will be missing."

She had asked me several times to join her on weekend trips. The last time Mary invited me to Aspen and I turned her down, she ended up with a new boyfriend which put any chances of us having any relationship on hold. I couldn't take that chance again. And something even more frightening, if I said no maybe she would never ask me again.

"Yes, I will be there," jumped out of my mouth. I really liked being with her and who knows how long it would be before I got another chance. After a very quick, "I will see you later," I went back to my treasure hunt for the retreat's packing list.

It took me over forty-five minutes to find the paper I was looking for. I went upstairs and expertly packed my black airline roll-a-board with what I would need for a night in the scenic mountains of Colorado and five more nights at a retreat in British Columbia.

I quickly dressed for an autumn evening in Aspen, loaded my roll-a-board into my Ford pickup truck and ventured out on a three hour and thirty-minute drive. It was a gorgeous afternoon for a drive, the sun was shining, and not a cloud in the sky. I cranked up some country music on the stereo, leaned the seat back, and settled in for what I knew would be a peaceful and scenic drive.

The trees in the city were still draped with the green in summer. They were beautiful against the bright blue afternoon skies. The ones in the mountains were glistening with the gold aspens. I was excited to see Mary and happy to be in the mountains.

There was barely any traffic on the drive which made it extra pleasant. The time seemed to pass very quickly as I concentrated on the tight turns on the mountain passes. As I got closer to Mary and my destination, there was even more evidence of autumn speckled throughout the mountainside with the changing aspen trees. It was a special treat to smell the fresh mountain air and see the changing trees. I loved having this time to enjoy nature in a way that only Colorado offers.

My excitement was growing, but what I didn't know was what Mary was thinking or feeling. As I got closer, I thought more about our conversation on the bench in DC where she said flat out that she wasn't going to go into another marriage where she had to live a separate spiritual life. We had seen each other several times since that day, but we never had another conversation like the one we did at Carlos' restaurant. I didn't have to give her spiritual life a second thought. I wasn't the kind of guy that would ever keep her from her interests or hobbies. I was curious about her comment about marriage. I wasn't even sure I was interested in that yet.

I learned days after this trip that she had something in mind for Aspen. It turns out she felt like she needed someone who knew her well to let her know if she could trust me or if I was a good man for her. And that special person to Mary was her business partner, Beth. Mary had confided in Beth that she needed her to give an honest opinion of me and of what our relationship could be. Part of the reason Beth was in Aspen was to assess me.

I had met the last guy she dated before me. He was obviously spiritual or maybe more metaphysical. Even though he wore regular clothes, he wore jewelry of stones and leather that hinted of a more hippie type guy. He was into meditation, chanting, and even channeling. I had no idea about the details of his interests, but I knew he had greatly influenced Mary in expanding her intuitive abilities and her study of crystals and essential oils.

As I passed the Aspen city limits sign, I called Mary to let her know I was close. She was actually surprised by the call. I'm not known for being a slow driver and maybe that is why the drive seemed to go so quickly. It was just shy of three hours since the call I made telling her I was on the way.

The city also showed the signs of the changing seasons. The decorations in the store windows all hinted to autumn and the coming of ski season. As only Aspen can be, it was inviting yet a little bit pretentious.

Mary told me that she would meet me in the lobby of the hotel. It was nice to know I would get to see her in just a few minutes. As I rounded the final turn and I saw the Hyatt just in front of me, I remember just how beautiful the hotel was. I steered the truck into the valet roundabout, pulled my bag from the truck, and tossed the keys to the valet. I hand him a five-dollar bill and ask him to follow me to get the room number. As I walked to the doors of the hotel, I immediately saw Mary's smiling face. She was sitting in a well-decorated area next to the main fireplace for the lobby. She was in her element and just as beautiful as always.

As I reached in to give her a hug, I said, "Let's get this party started."

We gave her room number to the valet and hopped on the elevator to take my bag upstairs. Mary shared with me that we were going to a Mexican restaurant that was close to the hotel. It sounded great to me. She shared that they had the best margaritas. Better yet!

Mary's youngest son Riley and her business partner, Beth, were both waiting in the room for us. I knew both of them, but not very well. I couldn't help but feel a little awkward coming to spend the night with them there. But Mary invited me, so she must be okay with it. And besides, I knew there was a possibility for an amazing relationship with her. I could feel our unexplained connection pulling me towards her like a huge electromagnet. In many ways, I had no choice to be there, it just felt right. I knew I belonged there.

Just before Mary opened the door she turned and gave me one of her patented smiles. It helped relieve some of the anxiety. I was aware from our past conversations that Riley wasn't too happy with the last few men in her life and that he was very protective of her. As an airline pilot, I handled many stressful situations on a day-to-day basis. But this was different, and I felt a lot of pressure. I was sure I'd be sized up and under the magnifying glass at least by Riley.

As we walked into the three-bedroom suite, I wasn't surprised how nice it was. The door was right by the kitchen that was fully stocked to include all the appliances of home. There was a breakfast island that separated the kitchen from the living area. There was a beautiful fireplace, comfortable overstuffed leather furniture, and views of the mountains surrounding Aspen. Riley and Beth came over to meet us and after a few quick welcomes and other pleasantries, I put my bag in the largest of the three rooms off the main living space.

"Let's go to the restaurant," Mary shared, "I am hungry and ready for a margarita."

The restaurant was only a short walk from the hotel. There were a few people along the sidewalks and overall, it wasn't as crowded as I remember the city to be. I noticed everyone seemed to be quite happy. Maybe it was just because I was happy. The smiles on their faces were as warm and inviting as the late afternoon sun. Both the sun and the smiles helped me realize that everything was going to be fine. I had nothing to worry about.

When we arrived at the restaurant, I was very pleased to see the colorful decorations of a typical Mexican restaurant. They were so festive, but also extremely tasteful and inviting. We asked for a table outside so we could soak up the last few warm rays of the sun as it begins to set. The hostess seated us at table for four and Mary sat next to me, Beth directly across from me, and Riley across from his mother. We wasted no time in ordering the pitcher of margaritas for the table and a nonalcoholic drink for Riley. I glanced over at Mary and could tell by her face and her body motions that she was happy and able to leave the stresses of owning her own real estate company back in Colorado Springs. Seeing her this relaxed put me at ease. The authentic Mexican decorations all around us with their bright colors added to the festivities.

It felt amazing being there with Mary and for a split second I had thoughts of how just being with her alone would be spectacular. I brushed away the quick daydream just as the waiter arrived with our big goblets and the frosted pitcher of tequila delicacies. We toasted each other. I was happy to be there and feel accepted by Riley and Beth. At least as accepted as I could be by a sixteen-year-old boy, protective of his mother.

The margaritas began to flow as did the fun. It wasn't long and we were all talking, laughing, and enjoying each other's company. The three of them were telling stories and asking me about my life. The only thing bigger than the smiles were the huge goblets of margaritas. The food I ate was spectacular and the company was amazing. I was so glad that I was there. I couldn't believe that for several minutes just a few hours ago, I tried to convince myself I shouldn't go.

One of the things I admire about Mary is her awareness, and because we were having a great time, maybe a little bit better time than the neighboring tables might have preferred, she suggested we head back to the hotel because I had a long drive to Denver for an early flight in the morning. I also thought that she might be ready to hang out in the hot tub for a while.

As the four of us walked back to the hotel, we all window shopped along the way. Mary and I lagged behind, giving me an opportunity to chat with her alone. I shared with her that I noticed that there were only three bedrooms. That was something that I didn't think about when I agreed to come and spend this time with the three of them. I shared with her that I was a little uneasy about spending the night out of respect for both Mary and Riley. I had not picked up any strong opinions from Riley, but he was unpredictable. She assured me it was alright, and I finally allowed myself to just take things as they were.

On the elevator back up to the room, Beth shared with us a recipe for great martinis. Mary and I agreed that we would love to try them. As soon as we walked into the room, Beth began to expertly create a superb fruit concoction, the grape martini. We all sat cross legged in front of the fireplace and told more stories. We continued to laugh and enjoy each other's company. I didn't know it at the time, but the bond we were building would lead to a life-changing situation very soon.

All of a sudden Mary jumped up and said it was time to go to the hot tub. We quickly went to our rooms, changed into our suits, and headed out to one of the public tubs. I'm not sure if it was the margaritas, the martinis, or just being intoxicated by the experience, but I don't remember much about the time in the tub. I do know I really enjoyed myself and was happy that I made the trip. Everybody was respectful and understood when it was time for me to go to bed. I had almost forgotten about the two-hour drive and another two-hour plane ride ahead of me. Four o'clock would come early. and I was still not sure what I was getting myself into when I arrived in Vancouver.

Our bedroom was what you might call rustic elegant. The king size bed was covered with a large white comforter. The furniture was exactly what you would expect in a Hyatt. It was very high-quality with a mountain flare. It didn't take either one of us very long to rush through our nightly routines and to be in each other's arms. It felt good! It felt right. I don't want to share all the details, but I will share, one margarita and martini enhanced lovemaking will be forever ingrained in my memory. The most memorable part of this evening was yet to come. And would have a lasting effect on the rest of our lives. Neither one of us expected it, and I'm sure we were both just as surprised it happened.

We were lying next to each other, and I was holding her in my arms. We were silent, just enjoying each other in the intimacy we just shared.

Suddenly, Mary broke the silence with "I have something I want to tell you."

It had been just over a year since my divorce, and I immediately expected the worst. So many things that she might say ran through my head. But what came next, I could have never expected.

She stated with only certainty, "I see a woman standing next to you." And she goes on to describe to me in great detail what this woman was wearing. She described even the most minute details of the dress, her apron, her hair, and even the look on her face.

At first, I was speechless, not only because of this out-of-the-norm vision that she was having but also because Mary had just described my grandmother and told me she was standing beside me.

My grandmother died when I was seventeen and Mary hadn't ever seen a picture of her. In fact, we had never talked about my grandmother before. I was shocked, but very curious. I'm not sure if it was because what we had just experienced together, the drinks, or the accuracy of her description, but I didn't question her. I was overcome by emotion, maybe I was feeling her emotions too. Mary went on to tell me that this woman wanted me to know she is okay and is proud of me. I couldn't stop the few tears that were running down my cheeks as I told Mary that she had just described my grandmother. I expected her to be surprised or even shocked, but she seemed to be comfortable with this vision. When she announced there was more, I didn't know what to think or feel.

"There is also a little blonde girl with you," she explained. She continued to describe in detail this little blonde girl in even greater detail than she did with my grandmother. She described her blue dress, her lace-trimmed blouse, her white bobby socks in her single buckle patent shoes. She left no detail out. The description Mary provided was so exact and so real that I saw her vividly in my mind, and to this day, I think I felt her presence in the room. I was overwhelmed and maybe even a little confused, but strangely there was no doubt whatsoever in my mind that Mary saw this child.

Just when I thought it was all I could handle for one night, she whispers, "There is someone else. I see a little boy!"

In almost as much detail as she provided about the little girl, she describes the little boy. She told me about his brown hair and his rosy cheeks. She told me about his plaid shirt, jeans that were too long, and clunky shoes. Like the little blonde girl, I had no idea who this might be but also like her, I felt his presence.

I finally broke my silence. "Who are these children?"

She immediately said, "I don't know, but the little boy says his name is Tommy."

I didn't doubt. I didn't question. I just fell asleep with Mary and these three visions on my mind.

Shortly after my alarm woke me, I was off to Vancouver. The entire two-hour drive, one-hour wait for my flight and the two hours and twenty-five-minute flight to Vancouver, I couldn't think of anything but Mary's visions and how being away for five days was going to be impossible. I wanted to know why she had these visions and who these children were.

There was an added bonus. I hadn't wondered what I had signed myself up for when I agreed to attend this retreat. A few people at a workshop told me that I had to go to this retreat, and I just took their word for it, never knowing what to expect. Obviously, it could never top my experience from the night before. I'm glad I paid attention.

Moment of Reflection

It is important for us to pay attention to everything that is happening around us. Energetically, we are tied together with every person and everything. Because of that, we can learn about ourselves and grow through our interactions with them. That is why it is so important to surround ourselves with like-minded and like-hearted people.

We must be willing to question our beliefs. They aren't real, just something we choose. If we aren't open to new ways and new understandings, we will continue to live life the same way over and over even if we want to change. The experience that I had with Mary that night in Aspen was well beyond my beliefs. When I was younger, I never would have accepted what happened. We tend to discount things that we don't think are right or make us uncomfortable. But the biggest transformations happen when we are open to seeing things in a new way and step beyond old beliefs.

Chapter Thirteen
Tell Me Who You Are

You are guided on the journey you have chosen,
and you will learn along the way the path to
take and those that are there to help you.

The Round Table, channeled by Vince Kramer

The number two question asked worldwide is *Who am I?* I thought I knew my answer to that question. After all, I had worked hard to be, do, and accomplish my goals. I thought I knew myself better than most. After all, I had been involved in self-help work and personal growth since my twenties. After I attended Jack Canfield's seminar, I was sure I knew myself very well.

I was wrong.

We have been taught that who we are has much to do with the outside world and that our titles, jobs, and achievements define us. We rely on how others see us to shape how we see ourselves. We see ourselves as a father, mother, friend, pilot, or executive. We accept that our roles in life are exactly who we are. We take on the criticisms of those around us and define ourselves as smart, unflappable, serious, or lazy. We alter how we show up in the world by wearing masks to be or seem like others want us to be. We believe that this is who we are.

We learn to see ourselves in the way that others see us. The norms of society become the acceptable description of who we are. We accept them and get locked into the beliefs of society and we get lost, not in the world, but lost from ourselves. We are lost from our *real* selves.

If we begin to question who we are or feel lost, we look around and believe we are the only one questioning or doubting. We think we are the only ones with these feelings or these fears. We believe we are all alone. We shut ourselves down. We put on yet another mask, so the world doesn't see the pain on the inside. But we aren't alone in these feelings. No one is alone. I wasn't alone as I was about to see.

It had been a few hours since I left Aspen. I was tired. I'd only gotten a few hours of sleep, and I had spent the entire plane ride from Denver to Vancouver thinking about what Mary shared in the visions of my grandmother, the little blonde girl, and the little boy named Tommy. I was completely engrossed in trying to understand.

I hailed a cab after exiting customs to take me to the hotel, my home for the next five days. I still had no idea what I signed up for or what to expect. It had been over six months since I purchased this program, and I don't remember why I let anyone talk me into it. Especially because they were people that I had met only a day prior. Maybe, it was because it was so highly recommended. But more likely, I was meant to have my eyes opened to my purpose.

I don't think it was more than a minute after giving the driver the hotel address and I was asleep. I was awakened by a sudden stop that caused my knees to slam into the seat in front of me and my face into them at the very same time. "You have arrived," said the man staring at me through the restrictive plexiglass between the front and rear seats, waiting for me to open my eyes.

I glanced at the hotel entrance, it was nice but nothing like the hotels I had been staying at over the last year, going to workshops and seminars in search of what had been missing in my life. The facade was very plain mimicking a southwest motif in Canada. Definitely not what I expected; quaint but inviting.

I grabbed my bags and pulled them through the automatic sliding doors. I guess it was just a habit, but I walked right by the Illumination Intensive by Warrior Sage banner affixed to a table and right to the front desk. As an airline pilot, I am in and out of different hotels all the time, this was just another one. The young lady behind the desk looked barely old enough to work. I gave her my name and after fifteen minutes of trying to find my reservation, she asked if I was with the group staying at the hotel. After I shared that I was, she informed me that as a participant in the intensive I had an assigned room. In a very lecturing tone, she told me I could get my key and learn more about my roommate when I registered for the event, then she motioned to the table I had just passed.

As I approached the event sign in the registration area that I missed earlier, it hit me, *Did she say roommate?*

She did, and that should have been my first clue to what I was in for the next five days.

The next clue came fairly quickly. When I stepped up to the tables, I noticed that something wasn't quite right. At least in my mind, it didn't *look* right. The sign draped in front of the three tables placed side by side was very professional and business-like, but the ladies behind the tables were more like the hippies of the 2000s. They all had flowing clothes, and their demeanors were what I would call free spirit. I was confused by the disparity.

The name *Illumination Intensive* and this free spirit way of doing business had me asking myself, "What did I get myself into?" The question actually flooded my head, thoughts coming and coming.

Overall, it was a very pleasant experience as Angel signed me in, got me my name badge, and gave me a room key. She shared that my roommate would be Paul, a CEO from Vancouver. Although the fact that I had a roommate was disturbing, I was instantly relieved, a CEO! I was going to be okay. I asked Angel what I could expect for the next five days. She shared it was hard to explain but assured me I'd love it. I thanked her for being so gracious and took my bags up to my room.

It didn't take me long to get uncomfortable once again. As I stepped into my room, I noticed that it was smaller than a standard room. There was barely enough room to roll my bag between the dresser and the beds. *The bag rolls easily down the aisle of a commercial jet, but not between the bed and the wall?* It looked like I wasn't going to be very comfortable during my stay. The bed was no different. I was going to have to curl up to fit into a double bed. It didn't matter, I'm sure we would be busy eight hours a day and there seemed to be plenty of common areas in the hotel. I always check out the bed and I sat down giving it my immediate stamp of approval. At least, there was a good mattress. I was tempted to just lie back and go to sleep, but I was hungry and once I did lie down that would be it for the night. I decided to unpack, claim my bed, and then head down to dinner.

On the way out of the room, I decided to grab the literature for the event. I was glad I did, I would have the entire meal and the rest of the evening to get over the shock I was about to experience. It was mid-afternoon and from the number of people in the hotel I must have been one of the first to arrive. I ordered a glass of Canadian cabernet and a cheese plate as a quick starter from a waiter who could have cared less if I was at the table or not. Reluctantly, he managed a smile when I asked if they have hosted Illumination

Intensives before. It should have been another clue, but I missed it completely.

While I waited for my wine, I opened the folder containing the event information and materials. The first thing I saw was the schedule for our five days. We start at 9:00 a.m. tomorrow morning. Quite a relief for me, I'd get a good night's sleep, have a leisurely breakfast, and be ready for a productive day. As is my habit, I looked at when we were going to get done on the final day, 3:00 p.m. *Whew* I'd be able to make my flight back to Denver with a little stop built in to grab some dinner on the drive to the airport. And then I saw it, the rest of the schedule. We would end at midnight the first four nights.

What, were they crazy? What in the hell did I do to myself? Oh no, and we start at 6:00 a.m. the remaining four days! That is a fifteen-hour day tomorrow, three eighteen-hour days and then ten hours on the last day. Why didn't I research this before I purchased it? Or did I know? No, I couldn't have known when I signed up. I just couldn't have.

By the time I uncovered this horrendous discovery, the wine and the cheese plate had arrived at the table. I ordered another wine right then. It was going to take me two wines to get beyond this schedule. The wine was a bit sweet for me, but that didn't matter. I must have been hungry. The cheese plate was half gone before I picked up the folder once again. Or maybe, I was just afraid of what else I might find.

Curious about what we were going to do for eighteen hours a day, I started to read about the awakening and enlightening experience where we were supposed to "get in touch with reality." This sounded like what Mary had been sharing with me. Maybe there was a reason I was there. Maybe, it would make a difference in our relationship. A new level of acceptance started to develop. I was ready to end this discovery process with that hope and put the literature down for the rest of my meal.

I finished my two glasses of wine, had a nice dinner, and returned to the room. I was exhausted after my short night and long day to the point I couldn't keep my eyes open any longer. Coupled with my concerns about what I had unknowingly agreed to be a part of the next five days, I was ready for this day to be over. Fifteen minutes after I walked back into my room, I was asleep. In those fifteen minutes, I finished unpacking, had a phone conversation with Mary, finished my nightly routine, and put a note on the door for my CEO roommate.

I was startled by my alarm at 6:30. I must have been tired because I don't think I moved an inch all night. There in the other bed next to mine was a man. He didn't move or look up. I was sure it was Paul, but I never heard him come in. As quiet as possible, I showered, dressed, and headed down to breakfast. When I returned to the room to get my journal and pen, Paul was already gone. Maybe I'd meet him later.

As I wandered into the meeting room, I noticed that there were about two hundred chairs set up in ten rows. It was theater-type seating with two sections and an aisle down the middle. The intensive was going to start in five minutes and about eighty percent of the seats were taken. Unlike many of the workshops I'd attended, about 30 percent were men. I was used to less than 10 percent. It was refreshing to have so many more males here in comparison. It helped me get into a more positive mindset and I felt something good was going to come from my time there.

As I looked around, my fellow participants seemed to be a smattering of every social and economic group. I felt comfortable around all types of people and knew that I could make some meaningful connections in the group.

The man to my left was about thirty-eight. He was from California and with his friend, an attractive lady in her early thirties. He shared this was his first time at one of the workshops, but his friend had been to one other. He, like me, wasn't quite sure what to expect. I could tell from his constant talking and squirming around in his chair that he was more nervous than me. To my right was a lady about ten years older than me. She told me that she couldn't wait to get started. She was at the same event six months earlier and it changed her life.

"What is going to happen?" I asked her.

"Oh, I can't tell you. You will see soon enough." she squealed with excitement.

The first session of the intensive started right on time. A man and a woman walked on stage to loud, upbeat music. They introduced themselves as Steven and Virginia. They were husband and wife. They had been with the company founded by the producer of the event for many years. The introduction included the rules of the event. I'll give the big ones.

First, no cell phones for the entire five days. We could call home and let our loved ones know at the first break. After that, we were to turn off the phones and not turn them back on until after the workshop. They also shared an emergency number to give our families in case they absolutely needed to contact us.

Second, we would eat all our meals together and they would be vegetarian. I knew why the waiter wasn't too excited about having us at the hotel.

Third, there would be two types of tables at our meals. We would be free to sit at the table we chose, but there would be only enough chairs for the group. If one type of table was full, we would have to sit at the other. There would be an equal number of tables where there would be complete silence and tables where we were free to talk only about the workshop.

Fourth, there was to be no talking between the time we were released at midnight and when we reported for breakfast at 6:00 a.m. We weren't supposed to talk to our roommates or anyone else in the hotel except to be polite. Lunch would be at noon every day with dinner at 6:00 p.m..

I am a very disciplined person. I was challenged just by hearing the rules. To top it all off, I paid for this! Steven and Virginia delivered the material in the first hour together bouncing back and forth in who presented. They shared with us different thoughts and beliefs on spirituality. They told us their goal and now our goal was to open up to ourselves spiritually and become more enlightened. Thanks to Mary, I understood these concepts although I wasn't sure I was ready or willing to accept them or make them my own.

The second hour was just as intense. They taught us the concept of the dyad. A dyad is two people sitting facing each other and completing the task assigned to them. I had participated in dyads before, but not in the way they shared and definitely not with all the intensity. Steven and Virginia were intense people normally, but when they were sharing about dyads they were over the top. I wanted to get it right to please them but also not upset them. During this hour they illustrated what they wanted us to take away from our time with them. They each took fifteen minutes and shared their perception of each other that was discovered through the honest speaking and concentrated listening that we were about to use. It would be challenging. I could see how the world would be different if we all learned to know each other at that level.

After fully explaining what was expected of us in a dyad, they demonstrated.

We would each be paired with someone different each session. We would sit in chairs facing each other with our knees about ten inches apart. Each dyad session was to be twenty minutes long. The first ten minutes, partner A asks partner B, "Tell me who you are." That is the only statement we could say to the other person. In fact, except for "thank you" that is the only thing we could say while being the asking member of the dyad. Yes, that is the only statement we would respond with for five days of these one-on-one dyads.

Partner B would state the answer that comes to them. Then partner A asks the question again. This repeats until the ten-minute point and then switch roles for the next ten minutes.

At the end of the twenty minutes, we would move to another chair across from another complete stranger and start the process all over again. We would do three dyads in a row and then take a fifteen-minute break before we came back and repeated the process. During the breaks, we could take care of our physical needs or walk around outside. All of this was to be in complete silence. Then we would come back for three more dyads.

All our days would follow the same schedule and routine every day except the last day. Here was how they were scheduled. We would eat breakfast at 6:00 a.m. It was porridge or basically oatmeal with dried fruit and nuts available. We would then have two hours of education mostly on spiritual concepts and ways to better do our dyads. Then dyads and walking, followed by lunch at noon. We would resume our dyads at 1:00 p.m. with a break for dinner at 6:00 p.m. We'd start again at 7:00 p.m. with a snack break at 9:00 p.m. before dyads until 12:00 a.m. All the time answering the prompt "Tell me who you are." It was going to be a challenge, but I was determined to follow the rules and get as much out of it as I could. At least I planned to follow most of them. I felt like I was in boot camp once again. Just like boot camp, sleep deprivation was used to break people down. But the food was better in boot camp, and they paid me to be there.

The dyads on the first day for me were repetitive and I felt like mine were disappointedly unproductive. Even though I'm not sure what *productive* would have looked like. My answers to the question were, I'm a pilot, a son, a husband, a learner, etc. All of my answers seemed to be surface level answers. Steven and Virginia said to say the first thing that comes to your mind. And that is all that came.

We were all in one large room, just shy of two hundred people answering the question "Tell me who you are?" I couldn't help thinking that I was doing something wrong when I heard people screaming, sobbing, and getting angry. I asked myself if I was missing something, doing something wrong, or if there was something wrong with me.

By midnight on that first day, I was ready to be done. I was completely exhausted, nothing left. I was hungry. It was definitely not the kind of food I was used to eating. The last time I felt this way was POW training in the Air Force. The difference was I wanted to go back the next day at the Intensive. Even one day of POW training was too much. When I finally made it to my room, I just wanted to go to bed. Paul was already there. Politely, I introduced myself. He responded by giving me the universal sign of being quiet followed by a zipping his lip sign. *Whatever!* I brushed my teeth and collapsed.

Day two started with people sharing their experiences from the prior day. They talked about anger towards their parents. Others shared about feeling free. Others said that they felt an energy in their bodies. I was nowhere close to having anything happen to me like these people were describing. The pilot in me came out. I was going to master this today. I was going to have an opening. Unfortunately, none of this I could *make* happen.

Steven and Virginia spent the next hour sharing how we could be more open and receptive to the experience. They talked about getting out of our own way. They gave us examples of how we were getting in the way. I know they weren't talking about me specifically, but they could have been. After our training for the day, we started our dyads. It seemed like it was going to be another day with the same results. I was frustrated, tired, and felt a little jealousy towards those who were having their emotional experiences. Even though it was obvious some of the experiences were made up, I wanted one.

And then it happened. I didn't have an experience, but the girl I was working with broke the rules. She leaned over to me and looked me directly in the eyes and said, "Do you know that there is a little blonde girl, with a blue dress standing beside you?"

My jaw dropped and almost immediately I whispered, "Could you say that again?"

She repeated, "Did you know there is a little blonde girl standing beside you?"

My thoughts were darting around in my head like wasps around their nest when agitated. Question after question and thought after thought. *What? Where? How? Why? It can't be!* I didn't understand. I wanted to believe, and I wanted to deny it. *Wow this is amazing!* and *This can't be happening! It can't be.* It wasn't what I expected. But I couldn't deny it happened. I was shocked, but I knew I had to break the rules. I was going to call Mary and tell her about the little blonde girl. I was energized the rest of the day and couldn't wait for midnight to call her.

The rest of the day was a repeat of the first day's dyads. Looking back now, it was probably because I was in my head about the experience of the little blonde girl. I just couldn't get out of the way, and it created a lot of resistance.

Midnight finally arrived and I skipped taking the elevator. I was anxious to call Mary and the line was way too long. Paul was already in the room. I don't know how he did it, but it added to me being anxious knowing I would have to wait longer to talk with Mary. I tried the basic pleasantries with Paul, but he just shook his head and turned away from me. That was fine with me. My head was still spinning from earlier in the day and I wanted to concentrate on the little blonde girl. I thought about the lady from the dyad. *How could it be that she saw this blonde girl next to me? What did it mean? Who is this little girl?* All these questions kept popping up in my head, one after another over and over. It took me twice the normal time to brush my teeth because I kept stopping and staring at myself in the mirror as I tried to make sense of it all.

I turned off the bathroom lights, climbed into my bed, and waited. Finally, I heard Paul snoring lightly. I pulled the blankets up over my head like I did when I was ten and didn't want anyone to see my flashlight on as I finished a chapter in my latest Louis L'Amour book. I dialed Mary's number as quietly as I could on my old flip phone. Hoping as the phone rang that she wouldn't be upset that I was calling her at 1:30 in the morning.

And then I heard her voice "Hello?"

"Hi, it's me," I said as quietly as I thought I could without Paul hearing me, "I know it's late."

"How are you?" she asked. "Is everything alright?"

Too excited to whisper, my voice got a little louder than I wanted a few times. I heard Paul stir in the next bed.

I had made a commitment at the beginning of the intensive to not make any calls, but I had to speak with her. Something was happening to me, and it felt like she was the one that held the key to my understanding. But also, in my commitment I owed it to Paul to not break the space he had agreed to as well. I was very quiet when she answered. I explained I couldn't talk very long, but I just had to feel that connection and see if she could give me any answers.

"I'm tired, but I'm fine." I admitted with the excitement of telling her grew.

"I thought you couldn't call me!" she reminded me half asleep.

"I can't but you have to know strange things are happening here. You won't believe it," I whispered.

"Like what?" she said more awake after hearing my excitement.

"People are seeing the little blonde girl standing next to me, in my aura," I blurted out.

"That's amazing! Oh my God! This is too cool," she shared.

I interrupted her as Paul began to stir, "I shouldn't be on the phone, my roommate is starting to wake up." I continued, "But Mary, I want answers, no I *need* answers. This is freaking me out."

She laughed and said, "I'll tell you all about it when you get home. Don't get in trouble! Keep up the good work!"

She didn't seem as surprised as me. And as I thought about it, I didn't expect her to be. We had just a few minutes to share what had happened in the remarkable parts of my dyad experiences so far. As we wished each other good night, I hoped I would be talking to her soon. Something had shifted in our relationship. I was still thinking of the little blonde girl as I fell asleep.

The next morning went extremely fast, and I hadn't thought of the events of the day before at all. I had just finished the first part of my third dyad. My partner, Beth, for this dyad, just had a breakthrough. When I asked her, "Tell me who you are?"

She said in the voice of a young child, "I am a rape victim," and the tears began to flow.

I replied with "Thank you" as we were instructed to do.

She continued to sob for the last few minutes of her time. Although I found it hard and I wanted to make everything alright, I just said thank you two more times.

Something changed for me after my experience with Beth. Her vulnerability opened me up.

"Tell me who you are," she asks.

As I stared into her eyes, I saw myself. They told us this would happen, I guess I didn't understand what they meant.

"I am questioning," I responded.

She followed with "Thank you, tell me who you are?"

My reply, "Alone."

My answers weren't profound for the rest of our session, but they were real. When the staff announced dyad complete, I hugged Beth and thanked her for sharing with me. She did the same and then confessed just before she heard the words "rape victim" in her head she had a vision of me with a little blonde girl on a wooden horse. And then, she just turned and walked away. Immediately, there was a tightness in my chest and a few tears uncomfortably rolled down my cheeks. I was no longer freaked out but still very curious about this little blonde girl. Somehow, she had touched my heart, and I didn't even know that she was real.

The structure and the rigidness of the days had already become acceptable. I had begun to be honest with myself thanks to Beth's vulnerability, I began to look forward to each new partner and dyad. The second little blonde girl sighting had grabbed my attention even more, but at least in that moment I wasn't obsessing about her.

During lunch, I sat down next to a friend that I made at the event where I was convinced to sign up for this Illumination Intensive. We were at a "talking" table and I asked her how her dyads were going.

Amy went into a long explanation, "Oh it is so amazing. I have uncovered so much. I've learned that I am important and have big things to accomplish in the world. I am meant to change lives." She continued, "I have had an awakening experience." I smiled and congratulated her on finding all these amazing things about herself.

Inside, I was questioning if she had really experienced what she said. She didn't seem to be different. She seemed just the same to me. I quickly stopped thinking about her and began to question the little blonde girl all over again. *What does it mean? Who is she?* The questions in my head came flooding back. I was ready for lunch to be over so I could get back to the dyads. I was being pulled to open up, to answer more questions, and get to know "Who I am."

Just two days ago, I was ready to leave. But this day, I wanted to know more. I not only wanted to know more about the little blonde girl, but I also wanted to know more about me. For the rest of my time there, I was going to sit down at an empty pair of chairs and see who sat down across from me. This wasn't a conscious decision; this is something I felt I needed to do.

I was one of the first people back in the main ballroom after lunch. No one had picked a place to sit yet, so every chair in the room was available. I made my way through the maze of chairs looking for the one that felt right to me. I quickly went to a set of chairs towards the middle of the room and sat down. There was a stream of people filing into the room silently. As the room began to fill up, I noticed everyone seemed to be avoiding the chair across from me. In fact, they weren't even making eye contact. I guessed they thought if they looked at me, they might have to sit down in the chair in front of me. Normally a very confident person, I started to wonder if it is something about me. I remembered our facilitators, Steven and Virginia sharing about those feelings on day two.

Finally, a gentleman about ten years older than me with graying sideburns and a gentle smile sat down on the chair facing me. I felt relieved; a sigh released from my body unconsciously. The paper name tag peeling away from the left side of his chest said Bob in a scribbled script font. Bob volunteered to go first, that was fine with me. This was my first dyad of this unusual event with a male and there was some hesitance as I questioned silently what I should expect. I don't know why I was so concerned; I was male, and it was no different for me than any of the ladies I've been paired with the last few days.

Bob answered the question, "Tell me who you are?" very similarly to the way I had been. There was no hesitation, but it was surface and safe. After each of his answers I said thank you. As I listened to his answers, I felt in my body and somehow knew in my mind that he had other answers that he wasn't comfortable sharing. I realized he was holding back. There was so much more ready for him to share, but he couldn't. Maybe he felt vulnerable, maybe he was scared, maybe it wasn't what men do in the rules and definitions of life. I flashed back to the day Mary asked me what the driver of the Camaro was showing me about me. I was seeing myself in Bob. Although I was supposed to be giving him my full attention, I wandered off to my tweens and I distinctly heard my grandfather's voice in my head. "Men don't show their emotions; never be vulnerable."

I'm tired of living by his rules, I want to be different. I want to help Bob do the same.

As Bob finished answering the question yet again. I said, "Thank you," and I really meant it.

It was my turn and this time I was going to show up fully. I closed my eyes and dug deep, listening for my truth. The answers came fast and easy. Was it because I was tired? Or maybe because I had been eating like a rabbit for three days? More than likely because I decided to be honest with myself and this man who was stuck with the rules of our past just like I'd been. I didn't know and it didn't matter.

"I am lost." "I am sad." "I am tired." "I am confused."

The answers came as fast as a machine gun. And Bob's questions and thank yous came just as fast. At the end of my ten minutes, I was exhausted. But I felt a certain lightness, a freedom. It was time for our fifteen-minute break, and I was ready for our walk in nature. For the first time in three days, I didn't think about anything but my answers from the last session with Bob as I wondered *Who am I, really?*

The rest of the day was much of the same. My answers were getting deeper, more personal, and I was being more honest with myself. Even though it had been explained more than once, I wasn't sure what I was supposed to learn or get out of these five days. And I was beginning not to care.

The third citing of the little blonde girl happened in one of the last segments of the day. I picked a chair in the far left back corner of the room and waited for someone to sit down across from me. Finally, a young girl about twenty-two slid into the seat almost hesitantly. When she sat down across from me, she was smacking gum and seemed disinterested in the intensive. She introduced herself as Skye. I agreed to go first and the very second we started, Skye stared deep into my eyes. I'm not sure what the difference was. I learned right then not to judge my dyad partners by their looks or actions. I felt seen and heard as I shared with her what I was feeling that was related to my mom. I shared about being misunderstood and invisible. I shared about being lovable and sensitive. This young girl's caring stare and clear blue eyes allowed me to see into my heart. I don't think I had been in my heart for some time.

When it was Skye's turn, she shared that she was stupid, slow, misunderstood. She shared that she was a liar and a fake. I no longer wanted to try and fix anything. I was finally listening without judgment and giving her a gift. Just like she did for me. About seven minutes into her time, she leaned forward and put her hands on my knees, looked deep into my eyes and told me about a little blonde girl she was seeing that was sitting on my lap. I asked Skye what the little girl was wearing. Her description left me gasping for air and grasping for an explanation, an understanding. She described her dress and shoes exactly the way Mary did four nights earlier. *Something's happening here that I don't understand. Something or someone is trying to get my attention. And it is working.*

For the second time since being at the Illumination Intensive, I couldn't wait for Paul to fall asleep, build my tent with my blankets to hide the light of my phone, and call Mary. I wanted to tell her about the experience I had with Bob and my desire to continue to get more from my time there. I wanted to tell her about what was happening to others. The shaking, screaming, anger, bliss, and undeniable joy displayed was something hard to explain. I still wondered if I was going to have one of these awakenings. I almost felt deprived. I knew she would be happy she wasn't with me at the Intensive

I was tired and I began to doze off, Paul was still awake. Maybe he was waiting for me to fall asleep so he could make a call. I would call Mary another time. As my waking hours were slowly coming to an end, I thought of all the spirituality concepts that Mary had shared with me in the months prior. I was beginning to understand. It was making sense, but I still wasn't sure why I felt that anything made sense. The concepts were still a threat to my religious beliefs, but I understood them in a new and different way. Maybe it was time to let those beliefs go.

Day four was a day I'll never forget. There were two more dyads where the women that sat across from me shared about the little blonde girl. Each describing her exactly as Mary did the night before I left. There was something going on and I was beginning to believe that Mary knew more than she admitted to knowing. Both women shared that the little girl was happy to be with my energy. There was no doubt, there was a message in all of this for me.

The most mind-blowing and heart-opening dyad happened right after lunch. My partner went first. Her name, coincidentally, was Mary. As I looked into Mary's eyes, I saw and heard myself in a different way. I asked Mary if she would like to go first, and she graciously agreed. I saw myself as she shared her answers. I heard myself in what and how she shared her responses. Each of my acknowledgments to her answers were heartfelt. It was touching and it brought tears to my eyes. Before I knew it, it was my turn.

I answered her every time she asked the question, but I don't remember the answers I gave, or I don't recall hearing myself give an answer. Probably because the answers didn't make sense to my rational mind. As I looked deeper into the eyes of the woman across from me, I only saw myself at a deeper level. All of sudden, I realized in every cell of my body, *I am everything and I am nothing*.

It wasn't just a thought in my head that was now void of any other thought, but I felt it in my body. I felt it in the air around me. This feeling, this understanding came as the time for the dyad was expiring. From the very beginning of the dyads, I had been hugging my partners as I said thank you. As I hugged Mary after this new and unique experience in the dyad, I started to shake.

I noticed the first two days of the intensive that whenever someone screamed or cried that a member of the staff would be there for them immediately. It was not so obvious to me on day three or four. But as I began to walk away from my dyad chairs, there was a man in his 40s by my side. I was now shaking uncontrollably. Every part of my body was shaking. My head was clear, and my body felt light. The only thought I had was a fear of something being wrong with me. I told the man who was obviously trying to make sure I didn't fall that I couldn't stop shaking.

"Just come with me outside, you are going to be fine," I heard him say, "You have had an awakening and have opened your heart," he continued.

I remembered during our monthly get togethers, Mary shared something about awakenings. I couldn't recall what she told me, and it really didn't matter. I have never felt better and been as scared as I was at that moment. This man was very loving and kind to me as he tried to explain what I was feeling, he escorted me outside all the time trying to calm me, "You are doing great. Everything is going to be okay. I want you to walk around the perimeter of this parking lot."

"But what do I do?" I ask.

"Just walk around the perimeter slowly and it will ground you."

So, I walked and I walked and I walked some more. I'm not sure how long I walked because there seemed to be no time. I do know that I walked all the way until it was time for dinner and didn't participate in another dyad that afternoon. I was still shaking as I walked to dinner, but nothing like hours before. It was euphoric; I had a clear head with no thoughts and my body felt like it was floating on a cloud.

I chose a table with no talking. I ate very little, and I left the table fairly quickly. It felt better to be outside in nature. The rest of the evening was a blur. I finally stopped shaking by the time I climbed into bed.

The next morning began on time, just like clockwork. Steven shared with us the day's agenda. We were going to have two hours of training followed by a chance to take part in other programs offered by the founder of the Illumination Intensive. After lunch, we were going to have a two-hour session to help prepare us to go back out into the public. Basically, they were going to help us close our hearts to survive real life.

I made a decision right then and there that I was going to leave early. I'd stay for the training and their offer, but I'd leave for the airport before lunch. I wanted to know about the little blonde girl, and I wanted to do it with an open heart. I hoped Mary had the answers to all my questions.

Moment of Reflection

I will never be the same. I was so resistant going into the intensive. It wasn't just that I didn't know what to expect. I knew at some level that it was going to change my life. I had committed to going so I never would back out. But I don't know if I could have moved beyond the resistance on my own. Because it was structured much like military basic training, the exhaustion and activity level slowly wore down any resistance that I had. As we got further into the program, I felt like I was finally getting to know myself and any lingering resistance was gone.

I went into the five days believing I knew myself very well. But as I answered the question and heard others' answers to it, my perspective changed. And in the final days I did get to know myself at a completely different level. It might sound cliche, but I realized, *I am nothing and I am everything.*

Chapter Fourteen
Little Blonde Girl

*What you see as synchronicities in your life are
actually two souls coming together to fulfill
their agreement to each other through
experiences of this life you have chosen.*

The Round Table, channeled by Vince Kramer

When Mary brought the concepts of her spirituality into my life through our conversations, it was hard for me to accept many of them. They were so different from my beliefs. I was still coming from the belief that if she was right then I was wrong. I don't know if I just didn't want to be wrong or I was afraid I had been living my life in the wrong way.

One phrase she shared with me was, "The Universe is conspiring to support us."

For some reason that statement felt right. It really resonated with me even though it pushed my beliefs. When we pay attention, we can see evidence of this everywhere in our lives. We can see this evidence outside of us, and we can experience it on the inside too. It can show up as a voice we hear in our head, a picture in our mind's eye, or it can play out like a movie in our daydreams. We can get a gut feeling or one in our heart area or we might hear a voice in our head.

When I shared earlier about promptings, I said that we receive these messages in many ways. We just need to be aware that they are coming, and we will start to notice them. We all are receptive to our personal promptings in our own ways, we just have to find out what they are. I hear them in my head, notice things that I normally wouldn't notice, get an idea or understanding in what others say or do, and notice as something lines up perfectly. Each person has a different way of getting these messages. Once they are revealed, a person knows then where to put their attention.

But it is not just about knowing how we get our promptings, it is also about noticing them. We have to recognize them as messages and not ignore them.

Once we recognize the message, we must believe it is a message. It is trusting the messages that encourages people to follow them. We are truly meant to get this guidance and to take any steps recommended by the guidance. Taking action is where most of us get hung up. But it is essential to take action as soon as the message is acknowledged. We receive the message when the timing and energy support our actions. If we wait or delay and the energy is no longer in alignment, the message goes away.

When our brain gets involved, we have a tendency to not believe or trust our promptings or wake-up calls. In today's society we have been taught to look for the reasons why something won't happen instead of the reasons why it can or will. This leads us to missing out on the creative process or just not taking action. We miss out on the magic of life.

But sometimes the message is so profound and attention-getting that one can't help but follow through. That is what happened to me when the little blonde girl kept showing up. It is the very reason I skipped the last two hours of the Illumination Intensive. I just had to know, and I couldn't wait.

I was counting the minutes, filled with wonder and anxiety. Only an hour and a half and I would be home. I called Mary again to let her know I'd be home a little after 1:30 p.m. I was lucky to get on an earlier flight. It is a benefit of being a pilot for a major airline being able to fly standby and fly in the jumpseat. I'd be home almost nine hours earlier than planned, and it still wasn't early enough for me.

Skipping out on the last session of the intensive where they close your heart back down enough to venture out into everyday life, hadn't affected me that much. At least, I hadn't noticed much of a difference. I was seeing things in a different way. I noticed people more and they seemed to be noticing me more. I was much more aware of myself, my thoughts, and my actions. The flight home gave me time to contemplate everything that happened and the opportunity to allow myself to experience gratitude and appreciation.

The drive home from the Denver airport was more pleasant than normal. I appreciated the crystal blue skies of home. Colorado has three hundred days of sunshine a year. Another reason to have gratitude and one of the benefits of being an airline employee is that people are able to live wherever they want. Traffic was moving fast and free. I glanced down at my speedometer and realized I was going fifteen miles an hour over the speed limit. I guessed everyone was in a hurry for me to get home.

As I approached the city limits of Colorado Springs, I called Mary again to let her know I'd be home in twenty minutes. I hoped I wasn't annoying her. I was extremely anxious. Not being an anxious person, I didn't know how to handle it. I wanted to know more about the little blonde girl, and I knew there was more to the story. Mary told me she would be able to break away from real estate clients about mid-afternoon and that she would see me as soon as she could. I was hoping it would be sooner than later. But then, I had time to stop at the drive-through on the way home. I was hungry and I hadn't had any real food for four days, especially not junk food.

The young man that took my order was very happy and delivered uncharacteristically great customer service. The lady who opened the drive-up window to hand me my order had the biggest smile on her face as she said, "It is so good to see you today, enjoy your meal." Maybe there was something to leaving early from the intensive. My whole day had been free and easy, and people had been so nice.

The house was warm and stuffy when I opened the door between the garage and the house and stepped into it. First things first, I opened the windows to let the sounds and smells of my hillside retreat float into the house. It had been almost two years since my ex-wife left, and it was still a challenge to come home to an empty house. I guessed that it would be an hour before Mary came by. I needed to do something with this anxious and excited energy. After I changed clothes, I put my travel clothes into the washing machine, emptied the dishwasher, and filled the hummingbird feeders on the upper deck that overlooked the pine and scrub oak trees below.

I knew what I was feeling was nervous energy, but I wasn't sure the source. Was it from wondering if Mary would doubt my experiences or was I concerned about all the experiences with the little blonde girl and what that meant? As a bachelor, I was lucky to have plenty of things to do around the house that I had postponed earlier to keep me 100 percent occupied before Mary arrived. A benefit of all this energy was I finished my long to-do list.

By the time she pulled into the driveway, I was ready to burst. I wanted to share all of my experiences at once. I refrained from overwhelming her and waited patiently at the back door for her. A kiss, a long hug, and a very sincere "I missed you" were the foreplay for the intense experience that was about to begin.

There had been no reason to worry that she might feel overwhelmed. We hadn't talked for four days and there had been so much that had happened. She is very intuitive and could see and feel the difference in me. I could see in her eyes that she already had a good idea of what I was going to share. She also knew that I was pretty open still and that it would be a good idea if I could ground some of the abundance of energy coursing through my body like an electrical circuit. Before I got a chance to share, she suggested we take a walk while we talked.

I lived about fifty yards above a historic scenic route that snakes through three tunnels in the foothills high above the city. We chose to walk on the road instead of the many nature trails, so we could devote all of our attention to each other and our conversation.

By that time, I was becoming impatient. As we took our first step out of the house, a conversation began, and it would last the entire two-hour walk through the tunnels and back and then some. I told Mary about my drive to the airport and how I hadn't been able to get the visions that she had of my grandmother and a little blonde girl out of my head. I shared that the plane ride from Denver to Vancouver was the exact same way. Instead of sleeping, I spent the entire flight trying to make sense of it all.

As I was reliving all of this with Mary, I noticed I was walking really fast and that was making her walk doubly fast. I slowed down and started to laugh. "You can tell I'm just so excited I'm practically running." I said, almost apologetically.

She laughed too and said, "Uh yeah! I'm the one running keeping up with your long legs! But I'm really excited too."

I went on, sharing about the Illumination Intensive event and all the rules that were required to be followed by the attendees.

"Can you believe we went from six in the morning until midnight every day?" I asked, still not believing it myself.

"No," she squeezed in before I immediately started talking again.

"It was like Air Force boot camp except the food wasn't as good or as plentiful," I admitted without thinking that she had no idea what boot camp was like. "We had oatmeal for breakfast with nuts and raisins. For lunch and dinner, it was vegetarian. We had salads and soups," I added, "I had to stop at McDonald's for some meat on the way home."

We both laughed once again. "It sounds like you just didn't get enough to eat, but it was probably good for you," she reminded me. "Especially with the type of inner work you did. You know, there was a lot of energy happening there."

I shared about the teaching sessions, giving her mostly the things that were different or out of our ordinary. I especially laid out the specifics of dyads and why I found them so effective.

Just as I was taking a breath, Mary was able to get a word in, "Yuck, that all sounds horrible. I'm so glad you did it and not me! It just brings up terror in my stomach to even think about it."

I laughed and said, "But I thought you were the spiritual one, remember?"

She instantly retorted, "That's the label you gave me, I just have a lot of knowledge about the Universe and the Ascended Masters. I haven't really done any deep work. Now you are the spiritual one!"

Wow, that took me aback. I was actually stunned that she said that she hadn't done any deep work.

Everything around us melded into our conversation; there was nothing or no one around. It was like there were three of us deep in conversation, Mary, nature, and me. I explained the progression of my dyads. I didn't remember them all because there were so many, but I remembered the important ones. She grumbled and snorted a few times as I told the story. I could tell she was really uncomfortable imagining herself going through what I had just done. I even wondered if I should tell her I bought us both an event ticket to go to a similar event together.

I illustrated for her the progression that most people take in the illumination process, starting from the surface answers like I'm a man, pilot, brother, and son when asked the question.

She just laughed and said, "Well yeah, what else would you have said, you are God?" I love that she said that because while I knew she was being flippant, I really did come to that understanding!

"Well, yes actually," I said with some caution. "The progression at least for me and the people I was with in dyads always got deeper and deeper."

I took a few seconds to look at Mary's face to see her level of acceptance. I remembered some of our spirituality conversations in the past and could empathize with hearing and ingesting what I was sharing with her. I walked her through the stages of answers.

"I can share with you my progression. It was similar to what I experienced with others. I started out with pilot, son, manager, brother. As we were getting towards the end of the first day," I continued, "the answers were more like I'm confused, I'm tired, and I'm searching."

I could see in her face that she was understanding what I was saying so I continued, "As the days went on, the answers changed to realizations that I was fear and love, pain and joy."

Mary was nodding in agreement, yet I could tell she was still quite happy it was me that had the experience.

"But the most interesting part, it all culminated for me when I realized, I am everything and I am nothing." I admitted as I found myself getting emotional.

I was actually starting to shake; my whole body was quivering. Just like the moment I had my awakening moment at the Intensive.

The shaking subsided when Mary shared, "I've heard that teaching many times, but I can't believe you experienced it! Holy cow! That's incredible!"

It was a perfect time to describe in great detail how my body, heart, and mind felt physically and energetically when I experienced my awakening. I told her all about the shaking, the feeling of something churning in my chest, I told her about the tears that just keep flowing uncontrollably down my face.

She stopped me, "How did they support you and help you through this experience? That must have been frightening."

I gave her all the specifics but explained that it was walking among the trees and the hedges surrounding the hotel for about two hours that assisted me in calming my body down.

"That was nature helping you ground the energy that was coursing through your body," she interjected. "One of the classes I attended in the past was about the energy in the body, the kundalini rising, like you experienced there, and how important it is to ground. I'm so relieved you had good people watching over you!" she said very directly.

After all the walking, my body calmed down further, but my mind continued to race because of everything that was coming to me, almost like a fire hose. I continued to share. I told her everything I could think of and then it was time.

"You remember the little blonde girl, right? The one you told me that was with me the night in Aspen. Just before the intensive?" I asked, knowing she remembered, but wanting to set the stage for this important question.

"Of course, I do," she said without hesitation.

"And do you remember, when I called and I told you about the girl that saw her during the first day," I continued with growing excitement.

"Yes, of course I do. Why do you think I cleared my schedule to be with you this afternoon?" she asked. "Hurry and tell me all the details!"

"There were four more people that saw her." I said excitedly and watched for a reaction.

"What? Please tell me!"

"One saw her sitting on my shoulder," I began. "Another one saw her standing beside me with her hand on my leg. Another said she was on a rocking horse. It all blew my mind." I continued without giving Mary a chance to respond, "I asked them what she was wearing and each one of them described her blue dress, the black patent leather shoes, and the white bobby socks. Just like you described in Aspen. They told me how she looked and what her facial features were portraying. It was mind-blowing!"

"What does it mean?" I asked after my ramble and almost out of breath.

"It is a sign," Mary observed, "that should be paid attention to."

"You know more about her, don't you?" I questioned her, already knowing in my heart that she did. "You have to tell me everything you know," I pleaded.

"Years ago, I had a channeling," she started.

"A what? What is that? What is *channeling*?" I interrupted, wanting to know everything she had to say, but oblivious to what a channeling was.

"A channeling is when the guidance from a higher energy, like an Ascended Master, is shared by a person who allows this energy to come *through* them and bring their messages," she continued.

"You mean like a psychic or a crystal ball reader?" I blurted out.

"No, not like…" Mary started again.

"Oh, never mind right now, I want to know about the little blonde girl," I interrupted her yet again.

"Okay, I'm delighted to tell you. I've been waiting all summer—actually the entire time we were just drinking buddies—to tell you about her," Mary said with great excitement!

Without realizing it, my pace had slowed considerably, and we were barely moving.

"My mom is the sole reason I had my first experience with trance channeling. The channel was named Angel. I don't know what happened to her. I met her only one time in 1992. Anyway, she was known internationally for bringing in the Ascended Master, St. Germain.

"Saint Germain? I never heard of any saint named Germain." I quizzed her.

"He wasn't actually a saint. That was his name. He is an Ascended Master," she quickly explained. "Bear with me until I share all of this."

"There is so much to tell you about that channeling, but right now what's important is what he told me about a little girl and that I was meant to bring her into the world in support of the world's growth," she began. "First, it was overwhelming, and second, I didn't understand much of it at the time, but he said she's the energy of the Divine Feminine. We can talk about that later."

That was good because I had heard of the Divine Feminine and Masculine in earlier conversations, but I never tried to understand it when I did.

"Anyway, St. Germain told me that a man who carried the needed genetics and energetics was going to come into my life and together, we were going to raise the child who would carry the energy of the Divine Feminine. Like I said, this information and this channeling really rocked my world!"

At this point, it was Mary who was sharing everything that she had kept inside. "He told me that I would leave my husband. I couldn't even fathom leaving. I had a six-week-old and a three-year-old. I couldn't raise them on my own and wasn't going to try." After a quick breath and a gentle sigh, she continued, "I couldn't imagine leaving my husband, until frankly I had met the man who was this energetic match, and knew that he was ready for me, my boys, and to have this baby girl!"

I was quite blown away by all of what she was sharing. But I understood why she didn't seem to be fazed by what I had shared with her. As she kept talking, I couldn't help but wonder if I was the man that this St. Germain guy was talking about. I wanted to ask if it was me, instead I continued to take in everything she was saying.

She went on, "Since there was no way I was just walking out on my marriage and no one appeared, I stayed married for another fifteen years! During those years, I was connected with another channel in Colorado Springs who brought forth St. Germain as well. That's another entire story by the way, but for now St. Germain shared that I could have conceived this little girl with my now ex-husband. But obviously, that didn't happen, and we grew farther and farther apart. And here *we* are! You and me, talking about stuff I have had to keep secret for almost fifteen years! He wouldn't talk about anything spiritual let alone something like this."

I was so full of questions, and changing combinations of fear, anxiety, and excitement as she told me about everything she believed or knew from what she was told or gathered during these channelings. It was obvious that she was telling me with the hope that I would at least try to understand and even believe. If I hadn't had the experiences I did during the Illumination Intensive, I would have doubted much of what she was saying. But those experiences made it impossible to discount.

Much of what she shared was new to me, but I had just experienced five people seeing this little girl around me and then telling me about her in detail. How could I not at least consider the possibility? Honestly, how could I *not* believe it? I continued to listen.

I was not sure what it all meant, why she received this information, or if I was supposed to even be a part of all of it. I wanted to understand and believe. I asked her about channels and the higher energies she was talking about. As she explained, I think I started to understand. There were so many things that she brought to the surface that I had never heard about or thought of before. I was intrigued and I wanted to know more.

No, I *needed* to know more.

As Mary finished, I was quiet, and she gave me time to digest this intriguing, yet challenging, information. For the first time since we started our walk, I was aware of my surroundings. It was Colorado at its finest. The brilliant blue sky was its signature. It was late afternoon then and the sun had already dipped below the tops of the foothills to our west. I heard the chirps, peeps, and whistles of the birds. They were joined in chorus by the bugs in their bushes preparing for nightfall; I was keenly aware of snaps and other noises coming from the forest surrounding us. It was all calling me to be present in that now-moment as I absorbed everything Mary had just shared.

As we approached our final turn and began the climb up the small hill to my house, it hit me: I wanted to experience my own channeling. I wanted to hear what these Masters would have to share with me.

"Mary," I said, "I must have a channeling. Can you arrange that?"

"Oh my God! yes! Are you kidding? Vince, this is a dream come true for me to get to share something with you that means so much to me! I will set it up and there is only one person living here now that I trust for your first channeling." She said with both excitement and obvious relief. She had heard me say for months that I was willing to try everything and decide if it worked for me. And at that moment, she believed me.

My head still wanted to get in the way and question all of it. But I couldn't and wouldn't let it. More and more, I had been discovering that I was being given opportunities to open my mind and heart to new ways. I was learning what spirituality had shared for thousands of years and that science was beginning to support. The way I saw the world and the Universe was growing, and I was expanding. I can't deny that there was so much proof in these concepts that were so new and different to me. We all have many beliefs that we have adopted from others that at the very least need to be questioned. So many of our beliefs have held us back and disempowered us.

No longer did I believe that we live a predetermined life. Fate was no longer the norm; we have choice in our lives and in our creations. My belief, understanding, and relationship with God had grown and expanded. I saw things in a new light. I saw them with my heart and not my head. It was stepping into the unknown. It was scary to take the steps, but it felt right. There was no other option.

Chapter Fifteen

An Undeniable Encounter

You aren't doing any of this alone. There are
higher frequencies, higher dimensions guiding
you on your journey. Everyone has access to
this guidance. You just need to trust and
surrender to the wisdom of the Universe.

The Round Table, channeled by Vince Kramer

Growing up, my beliefs and experiences were all in the mainstream of my conservative upbringing and religion. Like most, my exposure to things like psychics, crystal ball readers, and tarot cards was from TV or the occasional sighting at a local fair. And I avoided them at all costs. I'm not sure if I was told it was wrong or against my religion, but I definitely felt it.

There seems to be three camps when it comes to them. There are those that believe everything that comes from these mediums. There are those that see the readings entertaining. And finally, there are those that think it is all woo woo, strange, dangerous, or devil-like. When Mary first told me about her channeling, I fell between the latter two.

My mind was about to be changed forever.

First, channeling is much different than what I had seen or experienced in psychics. Where psychics, I believe, read energy and give answers based on energy, channeling is the higher vibrational energies coming *through* a willing person. We all have the capability to channel these higher energies in different ways. Some are more willing; some are more connected. I was going to experience a very connected person willing to allow my answers to be shared in a very direct way.

Channeling has so much to offer us. As long as I live, I will never forget the very first time I experienced it.

It was my first trip to Westcliffe, Colorado. I'd never had a reason to go there before. It was an amazing early autumn day. The drive down Colorado Highway 50 was especially beautiful as the leaves began to turn on the lower peaks of the Sangre de Cristo Mountains. The clouds were building and moving east, yet we were still basking in the sun through the open sunroof. Mary and I were joined by her mother on the day's adventure. As we passed the Royal Gorge, a Colorado landmark, I began to feel a little queasy because I wasn't sure what to expect.

Although I had asked Mary many times about what to expect and she had given me a very clear picture of all of it, I was still running possible scenarios through my head. I couldn't stop thinking about what it would be like. I wanted to believe, but I didn't want to believe. I wanted to trust; I didn't want to trust. I was a bit quieter than normal, content to let Mary and her mom talk. I think I knew that I'd just nervously ramble on, asking the same questions I'd gotten answers to before.

As I stared out the window admiring the golden aspens high in the mountains, I couldn't help but realize I was also moving rapidly into a new season of my life. Not because I had just turned fifty, but because I was seeing the world in an entirely new way. I had chosen to step into a new paradigm, and I seemed to be doing it in a single quantum leap. I was guided by the desire to find what was missing in my life. While the time period had been short, the results were many. I was encouraged by the circumstances that had undeniably changed old beliefs. Circumstances that I never would have expected yet seemed to be put in front of me in a way I couldn't deny or ignore.

After leaving the four-lane highway, we navigated the small winding country roads at a much slower speed. Soon, we spotted the mailbox that marked our destination. We turned into a driveway of a property laden with trees. Set off the road about two hundred feet was a beautiful yet peculiar house. It was a very normal modern mountain home on one end and an earthen house on the other. I had seen earthen homes before but never a combination like this one. It was such a beautiful setting with aspen trees everywhere and the house among picturesque outcroppings of granite and limestone.

As we approached the house and came to a stop at the end of the drive, I noticed statues of animals, fairies, and saints decorated the property. There were ornaments hanging from the trees that I can best describe as permanent party decorations. It was different than anything I'd experienced before, and the entire scene added to my wonder and uneasiness. It was very similar to my memories as a child of a churchyard decorated for a children's party. When I say *different*, I mean just that; it wasn't bad or weird in any way, just different. It was nothing that I expected to see. But then again, I'm not sure what I expected to see. The thoughts in my head were running faster and faster like thoroughbreds on a racetrack as we approach the front door. The butterflies in my stomach were all a-flutter, and the voices in my head were screaming. *What can I expect? A gypsy? A crystal ball reader? Something from a fairy tale?* All those questions were answered in short order.

Before we had a chance to ring the doorbell the door opened, and we were face-to-face with a petite blonde lady with a big smile that went from ear-to-ear. Mary had worked with her in the past and they knew each other fairly well. They hugged each other and reminisced for a short time. Mary introduced both her mom and me to this sweet lady she called Eloryia.

"Your house is beautiful, and I love the outside decorations," I said as I shook her hand.

"Thank you," she replied, "It is nice to meet you both. But give me a hug."

I had gotten used to giving hugs to strangers when I participated in the seminars and workshops I've been attending. After the hug, Eloryia offered to show us around the property.

She walked us around the outside and showed us her ceramic statues and a life size hand-carved wooden statue of Archangel Michael. He was majestic, standing tall on a wooden base holding a shield in one hand and his sword held high with the other. She took us to a grove of trees that surrounded a beautiful rock structure fountain that had a small pool of water at the base of it. In the trees were ornaments and streamers. It looked like the makings of a birthday party for a little girl. I think Eloryia could tell, I didn't know what it was all about.

"This is for the fairies and the elementals," she explained. I was instantly reminded why I was there. I had gone for a channeling which is just as foreign to me as the decorations and "elemental pool."

We entered the house through a door in the back of the house. The door was situated where the normal house connected with the earthen part of the structure. The temperature was very comfortable, and the humidity was much higher than normal in Colorado. I'm not sure what I expected, but the earthen portion of the house was beautifully decorated and was very peaceful and calming. The combination of the "a little bit out there" with the normalcy gave me a strange sense of relief.

After a quick tour of the rest of the house, Eloryia invited us to sit down for a cup of tea. I'm not much of a tea or coffee drinker, but I agreed to have tea with the three ladies. Mary and her mom, Joyce, had been to many channelings before and they suggested that Eloryia describe what I should expect. She said that we have plenty of time for that, and she asked us questions about how we met and why we were wanting a channeling. Mary shared our story in great detail concluding with the fact that this channeling was for me. We spent about twenty minutes in a conversation about why I asked Mary to schedule the channeling and the little blonde girl who was the impetus for my request. Then Eloryia said in a loving but very business-like manner that it was time to share about channeling.

She started by explaining that channeling is nothing more than her being a conduit for information to come through from higher vibrational beings. I think this is the first time I ever saw all of Mary start to show up. She was literally beaming. I was beginning to understand that we were doing something she really liked doing and it made her happy to her core.

She interrupted Eloryia, "The cool thing about Eloryia is she can move aside to allow these energies to speak through her. To get to speak one-on-one with an Ascended Master is like talking to God as far as I'm concerned!"

Oh, that is all, I thought to myself.

She shared that the energies that most regularly come through her were Archangels Michael, Raphael, and Metatron. I was familiar with Michael and Raphael from my twelve years of Catholic school, but I had no idea who Metatron was.

I interjected, "Tell me about Metatron."

She gave me a brief history and highlighted that at one time he was a man that walked the Earth, but now he is an angel and holds the vibration of the other angels like Michael.

Mary again interrupted and said, "He wrote the book *Enoch*, and he is in charge of all the other Archangels. He also works with sacred geometry. I don't know much about Archangel Michael, but I know a lot about Metatron."

I had no idea what Eloryia and Mary meant, so I just nodded. She went on to explain that there are many energies coming in for our channeling and she had no idea who might talk today. Luckily Mary had given me an idea of the angels and Ascended Masters, so this didn't worry me much. I was more curious about who had information for me and what that information might be. All that I had thought about since Mary scheduled the channeling was the little blonde girl, and whether I was going to learn something as big or life changing.

"Before we get started, I'd like to give you a choice of how this goes," she offered. "There are three ways we can experience this time with the Masters and the angels. The first way is full-body channeling. I'll get out of the way and the energy will come into my body and use it to have a normal one-on-one conversation with you. Second, I can just tell you what I hear them say like an interpreter would do. And third, you can ask me questions and then I'll share with you the answers they give in my words."

"Let me get this right, " I started. "For the first one they take over your body and I will talk to them just like I'm talking to you right now?"

"Yes," she answered.

"I want to do it that way," I exclaimed. "If I am going to do this, I'm going to do it all the way." And so, it was decided.

Mary said, "Awesome! I'm excited!"

"Let's go back to my office and get started," she offered.

We walked to this large room in the normal part of the house. On the way, she suggested taking a bathroom break. *How long is this going to be?* I wondered to myself. *I guess it really doesn't matter. I'm not going to want to get up and leave in the middle of talking to angels.*

We finally all convened in the office. *This is it, I'm excited and also very anxious.* It had been forty-five minutes since we arrived, and I hadn't thought about anything else. I appreciated all she did to make me comfortable in this new and challenging experience, but the anticipation was almost unbearable. *I just want to get started.*

The office was very comfortable and inviting. It was more a den than an office. It had a mountain-like decor with wood furniture. It was laid out in a way that there was plenty of space but felt quite cozy. I felt at home and comfortable even though the anxiety was at its peak. There were two windows on the far side of the room and a skylight overhead.

Eloryia offered Joyce a chair off to the side of the room and pointed Mary and me to a couch across from a high-back brown leather chair that had been placed beside her desk instead of behind it.

As Mary and I took our seats, I grabbed her hand. I'm sure I was looking for support, maybe even safety and security. Eloryia sat in the big leather chair across from Mary and me. A perfect hostess, she asked if we would like a glass of water, tissues, or anything else to make us more comfortable. *Tissues? Why would I need tissues? I just want to get started.*

Eloryia looked small in the chair; it almost swallowed her up. She asked one more time if there was anything else we needed. All three of us shared that we were fine. Inside I was screaming, *Let's get started already!!*

After pointing out a couple of blankets off to the side of the couch in case we get cold, she said that she will go inside to get them and see us later. Finally, I sighed under my breath.

And in that moment, it began: my first channeling.

As she closed her eyes, I watched her intently, not taking my eyes off of her for a second. There was a skylight in the ceiling that provided most of the light for the room because the blinds were all closed. Immediately after she closed her eyes, it started to get darker. I was able to rationalize that it got darker in the room because of the clouds that I had seen building over the mountains on the drive in. The clouds always move west to east as they come over the Rockies and I was sure they just moved between the house and the sun. I'm not even sure why I was so aware of the change of light in the room. I think I just didn't know what to expect, so I questioned and doubted everything.

Then, I noticed her facial features seem to be changing. She looked more masculine. Her posture changed as she sat more erect and leaned forward. I thought to myself, *How dramatic.* And in my mind, I also rationalized that she was a great actress to create these changes. She looked in my general direction and in a raspy deep voice said, "Hello."

Mary responded immediately, "Hello!"

I followed suit saying the same. *Wow, a really good actor!* I was able to justify my experience so far as this lady being an excellent actor and able to morph into her role. I didn't know what else to think.

She continued, "Greetings, I am Archangel Michael, and I am sure you are familiar with me."

I think I nodded, but at this point I may have been frozen. She (he) turned toward Mary's mom and expressed, "It is great to have you with me today." And then did the same to Mary. He went on to say, "But we are here today to talk with this young man," as he gestured towards me. "We have waited a very long time for him to be ready and have a lot to share with him."

I wasn't sure how to feel. I looked at Mary who seemed to easily accept that she wouldn't be speaking in this channeling. I found myself sitting as far forward on the couch as I could get without sliding off on the floor. I was drawn to the energy even though I couldn't explain it.

Michael looked directly at me, and I felt like he was looking inside me. He started and continued by sharing with me things from the recent past and how they had led me to this place and time. Over and over again, I was mentally able to justify what was being said. *Mary could have shared these things and Eloryia is repeating them.* I wanted to believe, but I didn't want to believe.

He continued by telling me that I have an important mission in this world, and I have lived many experiences to prepare me for that mission. He talked about my relationship with my father and the lessons he gave me. He explained the complex relationship with my mother and how it has given me an outlook of being a loving and giving person. He illustrated the importance of my first marriage and what the twenty-one years together meant for me in being in the time and space of this very moment with him. He shared about other relationships and their part in my current situation and in my growing into what I'm meant to bring to the world and accomplish. He talked about my grandfather and grandmother. He talked for what seemed like hours but felt like minutes. The entire time I found a way to justify that what he was saying came from Mary or maybe my conversation with Eloryia over tea.

I did notice I felt extremely warm, very similar to how I felt when I had the awakening experiences at the Illumination Intensive in Canada. I was confused, yet captivated.

Is this real? I asked myself in my head, not knowing if it mattered. Then I wondered if he might be able to read my mind. I was still able to justify everything he said, but I began to question that justification.

"We are here to help you open to who you are supposed to be in this world and what you are supposed to do." Michael stated.

"You said we?" I asked.

"There is someone else that would like to talk with you. Would you like to speak with him?" Michael asked.

"Yes, of course, I'm here to learn all I can," I replied.

I watched as Eloryia's body started to change again. I noticed her face and body began to look thinner. Her features become softer than with Archangel Michael. I watched as her posture changed. I continued to attribute it to good acting. I wouldn't be able to deny what was happening much longer.

She began to speak again, but this time, it was in a softer voice yet very much masculine. Her posture was more alert as she leaned in and said, "Hello, I'm Archangel Raphael."

He was a much softer energy, and I felt him in my body in a different way. *I don't know what this means.* I just did. I said hello back and this life changing—no, actually transforming—segment began.

Much of the first part of this conversation with Archangel Raphael was similar to the type of information and acknowledgment that Michael shared up until he leaned in a little further and looked me directly in the eyes. It felt soul-piercing like he could see right through me. He told me in that intense moment that he was going to be working with me for a while. I was not sure what that meant, but I felt in my chest that it couldn't be bad. Continuing to look deep into my eyes, Raphael told me that I am on Earth to open people's hearts and minds.

"To do that," he stated, "You, yourself are going to need to open your heart." I'm not sure I understood his words, but I felt his meaning. I was intrigued even more when he boldly stated, "and I'm here to help you. I'm going to do it with red-haired and blue-eyed people."

I immediately continued down my road of justification.

Mary knew that there were several red-haired and blue-eyed people that had come into my life recently including her oldest son, Lloyd. *She must have told Eloryia.*

And then it happened, the moment and the declaration that would affect me like I have never been affected and change everything for the rest of my life.

He looked right at me, right into my soul. I could feel him in every cell of my body as he boldly proclaimed, "As an example, do you remember the little boy in Walmart the other day? He stood up in his stroller and was watching you as you walked by. He wouldn't take his eyes off you and fell out of his stroller because he was watching you so intently and his mom caught him just before he hit the ground. He had red hair and blue eyes."

I was stunned! Shocked! It was a *Holy Shit* moment! There were only three people on this entire planet that knew this story, the mom, the little boy, and me.

There was no way I could deny or justify this. It felt like my jaw hit the floor. I glanced at Mary. Then I glanced at Joyce. I didn't know what to do or what to say. I was in shock, and he continued. He shared about ways I could return to the loving, caring, and giving person I was in my youth. He shared ways I could lighten up and not take life so seriously. He even suggested I wear a red clown nose in the cockpit of my airline jets. I was listening then with undivided attention as Mary continued to furiously take notes. He wrapped up by sharing that he would be talking to me often and Michael would be back to share how I would know it was him. And then he surprised me even further by sharing that, yet another energy wanted to have a conversation with me.

I once again watched a metamorphosis in Eloryia as she seemed to change facial features yet again, and her posture became more from a place of power or strength. This time I believed, and I watched and waited in great anticipation.

She then began to speak in a very deep voice similar to James Earl Jones and declared, "I am Ra, the Egyptian Sun God."

Ra spent about fifteen minutes showing how I would find things from the past to help in the work I'd be doing. He shared that people would come together to help me in the process of learning the many ways I would carry out my mission of opening hearts. I asked many questions like: Who I will help? Who will help me? What will I be doing? He explained to me that finding those answers are up to me to discover.

"Part of the journey is in the discovery of those essential parts of you." Ra explained.

I understood mentally, but I was disappointed that he wouldn't share the information. I continued to be a sponge though, soaking up everything I could. I had been absorbing everything that these three entities had to share even when I questioned where it was coming from. Sensing my frustration, he assured me that it would all come to me soon.

"There are many energies like me here to help you. This room is full of them. Would you like to speak to another one of them before we go?"

"Yes, thank you," I replied.

One more time I watched Eloryia change ever so slightly in front of my eyes. I'd already grown accustomed to these changes without any effect on me. This time her face was softer and more feminine. She looked somewhat Asian and very wise. When she began to speak to me, her voice was soft and gentle, very melodic. I asked her her name. And she assured me, it would all come in due time. She continued by talking about it being time for the people of the earth to move into a higher vibration. She went on by pointing out the catastrophes that we were experiencing.

"Floods, hurricanes, tornadoes, and earthquakes are happening everywhere on your planet," she pointed out. She went on, "You, as a society, have all the answers, and you can help the people realize it."

"How?" I asked, wanting to understand.

"The answers are in your science, and I will help you find ways to uncover them."

"How will you do that?" I asked.

"Don't worry about that for now. I will make it obvious to you."

"Thank you so much," I expressed with gratitude for this gift.

I asked yet another question, but she told me we must go, and, like Ra, she would be talking with me again soon and often.

I witnessed yet another transformation in Eloryia's facial features, and she began to look very much like she did when she brought Archangel Michael through. And sure enough, as she began speaking, I recognized the voice of Archangel Michael, the first entity to talk with me that day.

"Well young man, we feel that you have received enough for today," he said with love and understanding in his voice.

I felt held by his energy. The feeling was like when parents teach a child something for the very first time and not expecting anything from them yet knowing they will get it in their timing and do it well. I wasn't sure what the "it" was, but I knew I would get it.

Michael continued, "We want to thank you for joining us today. As we shared earlier, we have been waiting for this to happen for a very long time. We will continue to talk with you and share information if you like."

"Yes, I would," I blurted out, not wanting to miss out on another opportunity like this.

"We will come to you at night and help you remember what you all have access to in universal knowledge."

"How will I know it is you?" I asked, not even sure why I did.

Michael assured me, "You will know, and if you want to know which of the four of us is sharing with you at the time, close your eyes and look up. If you see blue it will be me, Archangel Michael. If you see green, it is Archangel Raphael. Yellow will be Master Ra, and red will be the feminine energy. Do you understand?"

"Yes," I say respectfully.

"Then with that I will go. Thank you again, we shall speak soon."

And with those words, the final transformation in Eloryia began. I experienced an instant feeling of loss in my body. It felt as if there was a hollow space in my chest. I was overcome with a chill and was cold. I was still staring at Eloryia like I had been for the last two hours. I hadn't taken my eyes off of her except to look at Mary or Joyce a few times.

I saw her face ever so slightly morph back into what I saw before this channeling began. The room got brighter, but I was no longer justifying anything. There could be no denial of what happened there. It was real. No matter what I might have thought in the past or others may think, this was *and is* real. I knew in that moment, others may never believe me, and I may never share the story. But it was real. I knew it.

There were so many things going through my head and so many feelings traversing my body. I was still questioning, but I knew that this understanding would change my life.

No matter how I felt about or justified anything I heard, I couldn't explain or deny the little red-haired boy. There was no doubt.

We aren't alone, we have support. There is help and we can get it.

I once again glanced over at Mary. I had never seen her look so connected. She actually looked different. I noticed all the stress was out of her face and any wrinkles she had were gone. Her eyes were bright, big, round, and symmetrical. I was fascinated by this. I thought to myself that she could feel the energy, and she was totally moved by the experience.

Mary reached over and put her hand on my shoulder. "You are soaking wet," she added. Sure enough, when I put my hand on the white striped golf shirt I was wearing, it was wet. I could have probably wrung a bucket of moisture out of it. It was still very cool in the room, so I didn't understand why my shirt was so wet.

The ladies explained to me that it was the result of all the energy that I experienced. I wasn't completely sure what that meant, but I knew that I had just experienced one of the most intense two hours of my life. Yet, when they asked me what I thought of the experience, all I could say was, "It was good." *What?* I thought to myself, but as I looked for the words there were none there.

I knew it would be a while before I could truly process what had just happened to me—to us! I definitely didn't know what to expect in the future from them, and I wouldn't for many years. I really wasn't in the room. I could hear the talking. I knew I was participating, yet nothing was registering. I know I politely thanked Eloryia for the experience, but the next thing I knew, we were driving on Highway 50 back to Colorado Springs and Mary was asking me if I was hungry. That question broke all of my silent contemplations. I wanted to keep running it all through my mind, so I didn't forget a single thing, but that wasn't fair to anyone else.

I was able to focus on Mary and managed to ask, "Why do you look so touched by the channeling?" Her reply and enthusiasm surprised me. This day may have been even more monumental for Mary than it was for me.

"Vince, you have no idea how long I have waited for this day. I have spent the last sixteen years of my life nearly alone in my spirituality and I was married twenty-five years." Through the emotions she continued to explain, "To have shared something so powerful with you and to know you did this to some extent *for me* just makes me unbelievably happy."

I could tell this was coming from the depths of her heart. "I had begun to believe I could never share this with a man I loved," she continued with such sincerity.

I was awestruck by what she was saying. She had never communicated such vulnerability with me, ever. I knew her pretty well, but I didn't know the depths of her feelings and conviction for desperately wanting to live a spiritual life with a life partner. And I also was curious if that meant she loved me!

I smiled at her and she simply glowed back at me. Her mom was in the backseat of the car, so we quickly changed the subject for the remaining miles to the restaurant.

I'd known it for some time, maybe from the very first time I met her in Cabo, that we were supposed to be together forever. The channeling and this conversation had solidified it for me. Just like the little red-haired boy spotlighted by Archangel Raphael, I couldn't deny the feelings I had for her. We were going to be together for the rest of our lives. The real question was how soon we would admit it to ourselves and each other.

Moment of Reflection

That day, I learned how important it is for us to understand energy and vibration. We have access to information and answers at so many levels. We are multidimensional and can receive and connect at these levels. We are so much more than we experience with our five senses. There are so many things that we haven't been given access to in the world, so many things that we haven't been taught, so many things that we have been sheltered from because of others' beliefs or fears.

I now know that there are three main parts of us where it is a necessity that we tap into them to get our answers. We call these three areas the "Trinity of You." It is essential to get answers from all three parts. It is also important that the answers from these three parts are in alignment, or they will create chaos and resistance that will hold us back. It will sabotage us.

I realize that for many, there may be doubts. For others, there may be questions of if it could ever happen. Others, I'm sure, relate to what I have shared. This was a profound experience for me. It was a real eye-opener and mind-opener for me. But I now know that this is just another way for messages to be delivered to us. We are all channeling this information and receive it in ways that we believe we can and allow ourselves to do. We truly have access to our answers. It is just learning how to access them in a way we feel comfortable. We have never been taught how, but it isn't too late.

Chapter Sixteen

Science and Spirituality

If you look at the Universe from an either/or
context instead of a both/and you limit the
complexity and the simplicity of its magic. When
you live from this duality, you live in separation
within yourself and from others.

The Round Table, channeled by Vince Kramer

W here I was most challenged in looking at the world differently were in the beliefs that are so accepted by society without question. Some of the beliefs I accepted included that we live a predetermined existence, things outside of us happen to us, bad things happen to good people, it is just part of life, and other people can control your life.

We justify being the victim because society and the media have taught us that we are victims. As soon as we accept being the victim, we lose our power. We begin to believe that others, fate, and God are against us. We believe that things are happening *to us*, and we don't know why. And we have the tendency to give up control. We believe what is meant to be will happen and then we stop playing an active role in our own lives. In some cases, we wait for the bad to happen and then believe we deserve it.

Scientists are starting to see things in a new way. They have learned that we actually affect what happens in our lives. We have influence on every circumstance we experience. In fact, quantum physics proves that we are the creators of our reality.

If we see ourselves as victims, we believe things happen TO us, if we see ourselves as creators, we believe things happen BECAUSE of us. As the split between science and spirituality narrows, more and more scientists are helping us to see just how much control we actually have.

We are truly magnificent creators. We are creating all the time. The question is, do we create on purpose, or do we create on autopilot? When we create on purpose, we can live the life we are meant to live. When we create on autopilot, it looks like things are happening *to us* and we are the victim.

As I've shared before, most of us don't know these concepts and we certainly haven't been taught them. But we no longer have that excuse. I know, and because I do, I am tasked with sharing it with the world. Where else will science help us understand life and spirituality? Where will spirituality help us understand science? I've found it is truly unlimited if we open our hearts, minds, and eyes to a new way.

Looking back, I see my parents worked very hard to make sure I had a Catholic education. They were both dedicated to God and to making sure we had every opportunity to know and understand the teachings of the church. Imagine the turmoil I was experiencing on the inside as I measured and compared these teachings with the concepts that Mary was sharing with me. They weren't actually that different, but they felt worlds apart. They were saying relatively the same things, but in a new context. It was a context of self-responsibility and self-empowerment. I was understanding the effect we have on each other.

Some of the concepts even challenged my understanding of science, which was especially true whenever Mary talked about the fact that "we are all one" and that we are the creators of our reality. Another extremely challenging belief she shared was that we *cause* dis-ease in our body by suppressing or repressing our emotions and by not letting our energy flow through our bodies.

It was less than a year from the channeling before Mary and I admitted to ourselves and each other we belonged together. We got married on a beach in Cabo San Lucas, the same place we met twelve years earlier. It was a beautiful ceremony with her boys serving as our witnesses. It was an amazing time in our lives. We were happy, and the time flew by.

I spent much of my free time reading and discovering other parts of spirituality that I knew nothing or little about. We synchronistically found intriguing books and met amazing people and teachers. As I continued my journey of awakening to so much more, Mary was by my side all the way. And she was right, I began to experience emotions that I hadn't allowed myself to experience. I had stuffed them in my body. As I was becoming aware, they were creating a lot of pain. My body was showing signs of major inflammation, but I couldn't stop. Mary and I were committed to learning everything we could.

The pain was excruciating at times and the results of the major inflammation were disturbing. One time my knee swelled to three times its size. Another time, my elbow had a knot on it the size of a big red apple.

Doctors couldn't figure out the problem and Mary suggested an energy worker, Diane, who helped me the most. She had previously worked with Mary and had exceptional results.

Diane was amazing and helped me in ways the doctors couldn't. After one extraordinary session, Diane asked if we would be interested in visiting friends of hers that afternoon. Mary and I were always up for a drive and meeting new people, so we agreed to go with her. We didn't know what to expect and really didn't care. It seemed like we were being led everywhere we needed to go since the channeling with Eloryia and we were sure this was another opportunity. So, we loaded into Diane's car, and we were off to meet her friends.

The drive from Colorado Springs to the northwestern part of the Denver Metroplex took us about two hours with the traffic. Along the way, Mary and Diane discussed spiritual and metaphysical concepts. I was challenged by many of the ones that they discussed. They didn't fit into the beliefs I held based on my strict Catholic upbringing and understanding of Newtonian physics. So much of this was challenging me to decide what to believe. It would have been helpful if I could have had some proof of these concepts. Little did I know that my wish was going to be fulfilled sooner than I could have expected.

As we pulled into Gregory and Gail's driveway, it was obvious that they had a different outlook than I was used to being around. There were copper pyramids, and metal sculptures of all shapes and sizes seemingly strategically placed around their property. It looked like the placement could be random, but it felt that each was placed in its location for a very specific reason. I was still holding to my mantra to be wide open to every experience, and only after listening and learning would there be any deciding if it worked for me or not.

We met Gregory first. He was a very nice man who was a true scientist. He was the shape and the size of the scientists I had experienced during my Saturday morning cartoons. He was very serious, and I could feel the passion for his work. He and Diane were good friends and after Diane shared a little bit about us, Gregory couldn't wait to show us around. He had been into sacred geometry for over thirty years when we met, and it was the basis for all of his work. Sacred geometry ascribes symbolic and sacred meaning to certain geometric shapes and proportions. Gregory created energy forms and tools to help others shift into happier and healthier lives. He is a known expert and speaks throughout the country on the concepts of energy, the Universe's effect on us, and his designs.

Gregory took us into his workshop and showed us how he designed and created one of his most well-known devices that provides integrative connection. It is a series of sacred geometric shapes encoded on a circuit board, using highly advanced technology, encased, to be carried or worn as jewelry. The devices were also energetically connected with strategically placed multidimensional forms around the planet.

He also showed us a system he designed to transfuse the devices with universal energy. He chose the stars, planets, and galaxies that had energies aligned with the purpose of the devices he made and used his patented method to infuse the energy into the device. It was quite a stretch for me, but Gregory's explanations and his ability to speak science and spirituality in a way that made the connection easy to understand had my full attention.

I was fascinated with everything I saw in his highly sophisticated processes and concepts. Gregory even shared with us some of his secrets. This was the perfect meeting for me at just the right time. I saw for myself that there was a connection between spirituality and science that couldn't be ignored or explained away. This wasn't the first time this had happened for me since I had been with Mary, and it certainly wouldn't be the last. They say time flies when you are having fun. It was certainly true this day.

It was late and we still had a two-hour drive home, maybe even longer with the traffic in Denver at 6:00 p.m. But before we left, I had to admire what Gregory had built one more time. I was enamored by the room that was fully inclusive and representative of his life, his heart, and his purpose. I could feel it. It was as life changing for me as anything that had happened. I had been given his gift of explanation of science and spirituality, and it would be instrumental in my understanding of energy and how we can experience things differently if we understand it.

Gregory insisted we meet his wife, Gail, before we left. Mary and I are firm believers in people coming together in partnership to bring their purpose to the world and Gregory and Gail are perfect examples of it. Too many people believe that there isn't a specific reason that two people come together in a partnership. When people find the reason they are together, they can each live their purpose while serving the purpose of the relationship. In fact, the same goes for an organization or a business of any size.

The second I met Gail, I knew she was doing what she loved. She was the perfect match for Gregory. It was obvious they belonged together. Just like her husband, Gail loved to share the science behind what they do. I enjoyed both of them so much, but we had to get back on the road.

As we were saying our goodbyes, Gail gave me the second gift of this trip. She shared that she couldn't wait to get back to her book that she was almost finished reading. I'm always curious about what others read and I asked her the name of it. She graciously shared she was reading a book on the effects of quantum physics on real life. Mary rolled her eyes when she told us it was a real page turner. I was sure it would be for me. Quantum physics tells us there are no mistakes or coincidences. I must read the book. I put it on my internal to-do list: Buy that book.

I was given a direction to follow and actions to take. It was truly a message I was meant to hear and pay attention to. This type of message or what we call *promptings* had been happening more and more often and they were happening almost immediately to us. I'd read an article in a newspaper or magazine about "frequency" and on my next airline trip there was a book titled *Frequency* on the counter of a store I visited. I learned about how we create and manifest and there is a Facebook ad for Dr. Joe Dispenza. Mary shared some of her beliefs and I found my copy of Jack Canfield's book when I was straightening a shelf in the basement. Jack talked about the importance of community and asking the Universe for what you want. He shared about the power of beliefs and the importance of compassion. No mistakes. No coincidences.

The interesting thing was I kept believing that these promptings would all point towards what I'd been taught and what I have believed my entire life. But the opposite was true. They all pointed to what Mary had shared. All of her concepts were proving to be true and are also scientifically based.

How could I argue with or doubt any of them? I was learning and growing, and I was being shown the way and led on the path to proving everything the Masters shared in the channeling.

Moment of Reflection

Hundreds of books have been put in front of me, all at the perfect time. I have followed and learned from some of the top mentors in their fields, people like Jack Canfield, Joe Dispenza, Debbie Ford, Bruce Lipton, Gregg Braden, and many more. All of it led me to the life I am meant to live, a life I'm still uncovering, and I know I chose. As I learn more and grow, I can look back at the circumstances and experiences that have happened in my life and see that I have been moving towards this chosen life in everything that has happened.

We are all constantly getting messages and promptings put in front of us to get our attention and help us grow and expand. There are so many things that we don't know that are keeping us from being our best selves, creating what we want in our lives, and making a difference. And as the saying goes, we don't know what we don't know.

We have to open ourselves to the unlimited possibilities available to us in the Universe or the quantum field. When we uncover and understand how energy works and how we as energetic beings can use that knowledge to create, attract, and experience our life on purpose. Science has so much to share that hasn't made it into the mainstream. And as we learn and uncover, we will create a world that is unrecognizable to us.

Chapter Seventeen
Like Minded, Like Hearted

*The people that come and go in your life all
assist you in your learning, growing, and
expanding. Each relationship is co-created to
provide the experience needed for you to step
into your chosen mission, your reason for being.*

The Round Table, channeled by Vince Kramer

One of the most important things that we need to realize as we start to understand who we are and why we are here is that we aren't meant to do any of this alone. We are community animals. We are meant to live in community and help each other navigate this life. Energetically, we are all connected. What we do, say, or think affects others. And they affect us. Quantum physics explains this through concepts like non-locality, entanglement, and entrainment.

Because of this, we need to choose our communities wisely. We want to surround ourselves with like-minded and like-hearted people who support us. When I say *support*, I mean they are willing to help us see those magnificent parts of ourselves, but also those parts that are sabotaging or holding us back. They support us in the internal work needed to heal those parts and in living the life we are meant to live. They support us in uncovering the unique combination of gifts and talents and in sharing them with the world.

Many of us tend to hold on to relationships that no longer serve us. When we do, we limit the space we have for the relationships that will and do support us. When we make the space to attract those types of people in our lives, we begin to form that supportive community which grows and expands together. A community will understand us and our circumstances, but not allow us to stagnate because of them. I found one of those communities with one of my most influential mentors.

I had been in the Jack Canfield community for three years. It was truly life changing for me. They say everything happens for a reason and quantum physics backs that statement up whole-heartedly. There are no mistakes or coincidences.

During my year in Jack's Platinum Coaching program, my life changed dramatically. It truly was a holistic mind, body, and spirit experience. During that year we had many in-person events which were priceless. The last of those events was held in Jack's hometown Santa Barbara. Our platinum group was relatively small and the opportunity to participate in one-on-one coaching with the author of the *Chicken Soup for the Soul* series was phenomenal. I really appreciated Jack and what he shared with the world.

The culmination of this Santa Barbara event was an evening reception at Jack's house in the hills above the city. He had become one of my most trusted mentors and the look into his personal world was exciting. I related to his sincerity and genuine desire to help others. It was in alignment with what I knew I was being called towards. I had so many things happen in the first three years in his community, and I looked forward to being in the more intimate and personal setting of this reception for our group of almost thirty people.

Our hotel was right across from the pier. As we climbed into the white fifteen-passenger vans, we could see the tourists and local residents enjoying the shops and restaurants along it. We were being transported as a group by several vans from our hotel to the house. The drive-through the city and up into the mountains was accentuated by the beauty of the scenery and the celebrity houses we passed.

Our group was full of anticipation. The chatter of several conversations about what to expect and how exciting it was to be visiting his house turned into a high vibrational buzz. Everyone had an opinion, and no one had a clue. As we wound through the hills and trees, it was fascinating to see the beautiful homes speckled throughout the hillside. As we turned into his driveway, I was not disappointed by the beautiful house awaiting us. It was inviting and charming, but at the same time it was grand and majestic. It exuded the energy of Jack and his wife, Inga. It was so welcoming, I felt like I was coming home.

Jack and Inga met us at the door and graciously invited us into their home. It was exquisitely decorated and very comfortable. It matched Jack perfectly. Much of Jack's staff was there also to enjoy the evening with us.

Jack and Inga divided us up in two groups to give us a tour. I was captivated by the crystals and geodes of museum quality that were on display throughout the house. One of the most beautiful was a five-foot-tall citrine cathedral that adorned the entryway. It was brilliant and the orange color caught the eye immediately. It cradled me in its energy, and I couldn't help but be in a higher vibration just being around it. This was my first introduction to crystals of this size and quality, and I sensed a connection and knew immediately that there would be some in my future.

There was another superb specimen of quartz crystal on the tour. It was clear and back lit which made it stand out from every direction. It had a personality of its own and seemed to be holding the energy of the house. I had heard about crystals and energy from Mary. Jack came across to me as subdued and conservative. I saw him in a different light after the tour of his house and experiencing his crystals. He was the person I most wanted to be like before I had my spiritual awakening with Mary's help, and then I was experiencing this different and intriguing side of him. I was curious, *Has he ever experienced channeling? Would he understand what happened to me? Has it happened to him?* It gave me a sense of security and almost permission to believe as I saw the spiritual side of him. After all, my mentor was showing signs of having a similar belief. I was encouraged and suddenly didn't feel so alone.

The second most exciting place on the tour was Jack's office. As a well-known author, he has accomplished a lot, and this was where most of it happened. I allowed myself to dream of what it would be like to make a difference in so many people's lives like he has. I felt empowered and believed it was possible when I was in the energy of that room. Like Jack, I'm called to teach and share. I'm called to affect transformations *for* people and *with* people. When I was in the creative energies of his home, I could feel them ignite in me.

I was having a wonderful time. I had spent a lot of time with these people during our program, but we had never had the opportunity to enjoy being together in a more relaxed setting. I felt that I had missed out on not getting to know them in this way much earlier. I was sure that we would have a connection many years into the future. The bond of community is so much more important than we realize.

Out of the men in the group, Glen was my favorite. We had the opportunity to help each other in many ways on this journey. He had become a good friend and an even better sounding board. I noticed Glen sitting at a small table by himself. This was the perfect opportunity to share some things with him that I could use some feedback on. I put together a hors d'oeuvres plate, grabbed a drink, and made my way over to the table where he was sitting. I enjoyed Glen. He was easy to talk to and I trusted him. We were having a great conversation. At one point in our conversation, I heard in my head, *Share your story!* It was a very strong message which normally would have terrified me. Instead, I noticed my body was quite calm. There were no signs of nervousness, and I actually had a wave pass through my body as I felt a gentle calmness set in.

"Can I share something with you that might seem a little strange," I asked knowing that he would say yes.

"Of course," Glen said without thinking.

Before I lost my confidence, the words, "I went to a channeling with Mary and talked to angels," flowed from my mouth.

I expected some form of confusion or hesitation. Instead, Glen was quite interested.

"What do you mean you talked to angels?" he asked almost nonchalantly.

I took the next fifteen minutes to share as much detail as I could about the channeling with Mary and Eloryia. I told him what she looked like, what they said and how I felt. The entire time I watched his face to judge the level of acceptance. I could tell by the quizzical look on his face that he had some doubts but wanted to believe.

"What angels did you talk to?" he asked, not skipping a beat.

"Well, Archangel Michael and Archangel Raphael. But it wasn't just angels. There was Ra, the Egyptian God of the Sun and a feminine energy too. They were sharing that they wanted me to wake up and start living true to who I am," I shared a bit hesitantly.

Glen listened, acceptingly focused on our conversation despite the distractions around us. It was refreshing, and in some ways relieving, to feel normal when discussing something so judged. I felt heard and normal although the topics seemed strange and out of the ordinary to me.

"How have things changed for you since these conversations?" Glen asked in hopes of learning more.

"It took me a while to accept and even believe it happened," I admitted. "They told me they would come in the night to share more information."

I continued to share about what had happened since the channeling. I was sharing with him about the voices I had begun to hear at night and Archangel Michael talking to me when I felt a hand on my shoulder. When I glanced back, I saw Jack with his loving, fatherly smile.

"Do you mind if I join you?" he asked.

"We would be honored," Glen and I shared in unison.

"What are you talking about?" he inquired. "I could tell by your faces that it is something I want to be part of."

Glen looked at me for guidance or at least a sign that it was alright to share our conversation. I appreciated that he respected my story and left it up to me to disclose if I chose. In what I'm sure was only a second or two, my hands got sweaty, my pulse raced to over 140bpm, and I became tongue-tied because of the adrenaline rushing through my body. I wanted to share, but I didn't know if it would be accepted. I had only shared my experiences with a few trusted people. But this was Jack Canfield. If he wasn't receptive, how would that affect me? I didn't know what I wanted to do.

I am not sure what was the deciding factor, if it was Jack's big heart, just my time to open up, or a combination of both, I just let it go. I shared about the channeling, the angels talking to me and seeing colors at night. I told him about my desire to bring science and spirituality together and to share it in similar ways to how he was doing it. I talked more openly than I had in the last several years. It felt good. Both men were sitting there looking at me in complete silence, taking it all in. I could tell by their posture they were totally interested and wanted to hear everything I had to say. It felt good to be able to share so openly and honestly. And I was sharing with Jack Canfield. I could see the understanding and the acceptance in his face. I was experiencing the feeling of purpose coursing through my veins, my purpose! It didn't matter if he accepted what I was saying, but he did. It was obvious. I knew we were on the same page. And for the first time I knew where I was going to go and the path I was supposed to be on.

Glen shared some of his deepest desires and how he planned to get there. Jack and I listened intently as Glen started to open up and share from the depth of his heart. I was connected to each and every word. I could see that he had a similar understanding of who he was too. It was extremely special to experience a connection like that.

When Glen finished, Jack told us that he was writing a book about his awakening and experiences. He shared about his personal connection with source energy and his understanding of his life's purpose. He shared what he saw as the journey in front of him. He shared his beliefs and how he came to find and understand them. He told us about how the book *The Golden Motorcycle Gang* was going to help people feel more comfortable and confident to follow their guidance and find their purpose.

This was an empowering conversation. I wish I could have many more of them. Jack gave me hope and courage. He showed me by sharing his story that I'm not alone and people need to hear my story. He gave me permission to forget the rules my grandfather gave me. He opened the door for me to share concepts outside the small box we live in. He helped me see I'm not the only one to be called to more. He pointed out that there always has to be someone who is willing to lead the way. It was a gift I will never forget. There was a connection of purpose that I shared with him. My mentor had come through again, bigger than ever.

When we are around like-minded and like-hearted people, we naturally want to be better, be more of what we know we are on the inside. When we find ourselves in the presence of people who are holding a higher vibration than we are, the natural tendency is for our energy to seek the higher vibration of that person. That is what happened with Jack. Learning and understanding the laws governing energy is essential, so we can comprehend the high and low frequencies of our vibration.

Moment of Reflection

I would be remiss if I didn't share two other concepts of energy when it comes to relationships and community. The first is being in the presence of a lower vibration. Despite what many believe, a lower vibration doesn't have to adversely affect us. If we choose to hold our vibrational level, the lower vibration will not affect us. In fact, the tendency is for the lower vibration to seek our frequency. But if people allow their vibration to drop or choose to go to the lower vibration, they aren't serving themselves or the person with the lower vibration.

The second concept is what will be experienced when around people with a different vibration: chaos. This is because the vibrations aren't resonating or matching. Being aware of the chaos will help a person see their given vibration and allow them to make a conscious decision on what to do with it. In this chaos, a person might experience unease, but they can choose to stay in the higher vibration.

Understanding these concepts will help people make sense of and choose the most empowering direction for them when experiencing others and their energetic vibrations.

Relationships and experiences like I experienced with Jack support us in raising our vibration and expanding into who we are, who we are meant to be. We are in a more accepting state and willing to accept and take action on our knowingness and promptings. We actually attract these people and opportunities into our lives to support us on this journey. Some would say, and I tend to agree, that there are actually soul agreements that have been made to help us awaken to the unlimited possibilities, choose the necessary steps and actions, and to willingly step into all that we are meant to be.

The choice is ours. We can look for the like-minded and like-hearted and accept into our lives those that we attract to support our growth. In turn, we will support and aid others as we move swiftly on our journeys. Or we can choose to be alone or in non-supportive relationships and need to have moments of choice to help us make the decision to get back on path.

As I climbed into bed after that exhilarating night, I realized that this was an important time in my awakening to purpose. It wasn't a new awakening but because of Jack Canfield, I gave myself permission to share it. My body relaxed, and I realized the tension I had been feeling was nothing more than the fact that I had been holding back from sharing my calling. Not allowing myself to be authentic had taken a toll, but it was different that night. The voices in my head, both the ego and the

Masters, were quiet. My body was relaxed. My eyelids were heavy. My heart was open. My future was clear.

I quickly fell asleep and dreamt of my purpose.

Chapter Eighteen
Messages and Promptings

*Pay attention to the messages and the
promptings you get. They are meant to help you
remember who you are and how to move
towards it. When you are aligning with the life
you are meant to live, you will get the help you
need at the time you need it most.*

The Round Table, channeled by Vince Kramer

We all have a purpose for being on Earth. Until Eloryia's channeling, I had an idea what mine was, but like many others, was searching for the exact words and an understanding of what it all meant.

After the channeling, I still wasn't sure exactly what my purpose was, but I realized it was bigger than I had ever imagined. I've learned that there are three parts to our purpose, and they are all just as important as the others. One of those parts is our energy that we bring to the world. We call it our *quintessence*. It is the real and concentrated essence of who we are.

When we understand what this energy is and align to it, we allow our messages to come more easily. This alignment of our frequency or vibration to our true or real self opens up the information channels for us to get guidance from a higher-level frequency. The message or guidance we receive is more easily understood and implemented into our day-to-day lives. Despite popular belief, we all have access to guidance to help us live our purpose. We just aren't sure how to access it.

It is kind of a quandary. The more guidance we can receive, the better we are able to live our purpose which makes it easier for us to tap into the guidance that is available to us. Through the channeling, I started to align with my reason for being. Because I did, the guidance was more and more available.

And the guidance kept coming.

"When you hear voices in the middle of the night just look up with eyes closed and if you see blue it is me," Archangel Michael told me.

I don't think I'll ever forget those words. Partially because I would never forget the first channeling that I had with Eloryia, but also because most nights I would wake up hearing the Masters. And most nights, it was the voice of Michael that I heard.

I woke up as my body went rigid and I felt what seemed to be a jolt of electricity shooting through my body. My whole left side shuddered uncontrollably. Initially, it was very scary for me. I thought there was something medically wrong with me. And then, when it began happening three to four times a week, I realized that it was the beginning of getting aligned to receive even more information that was going to help me do exactly what I told my grandmother I wanted to do, "Help people love themselves so they could love each other."

One night, I awoke, and something was different. I was soaking wet with sweat even though I was under only a thin sheet, and it was cool in our bedroom. My pillow was soaked all the way through. The bed was wet to the point that it was uncomfortable. I wasn't sick, and I didn't have a fever. I was just about ready to get out of bed and I heard a familiar voice. I had heard it often those last couple of years with the Masters. "It is time for you to open up to a new paradigm of thought," the voice of Archangel Michael stated emphatically.

I had never heard anything like that from any of the voices before. I closed my eyes and looked up just as I was instructed to do. For the first time, I saw two colors at the same time. I saw the blue of Archangel Michael, as I expected, and a magenta color I had never seen before. The two colors came together to form an intriguing shade of violet.

I was confused; I'd never seen anything like this before. It was like a kaleidoscope in my head. And then I heard a second voice. "You picked the time and date you were born. You picked the place you were going to live, and you picked your parents."

I knew the information was extremely important, but at the time I was more excited by the new voice. I asked the voice in my mind, *Who are you?*

And the voice said, "In good time."

The conversation—or more correctly *lecture*—went on for over two hours. Each of the voices shared one at a time mostly, but there were times that they both shared at once. Michael shared about living my purpose and that I had to learn about purpose before I could learn mine. He shared about timing and the importance of every experience in life. The magenta energy told me about lessons, transformation, and energy. It was a masculine energy that was very direct and to the point. As he shared about free will, it was obvious he was saying to use it, and I used mine to follow his suggestions. Just like every other night that I heard voices, I understood every word and the concepts felt right.

Deep down, I knew this information needed to get out and I was the one who was supposed to do it. And just like every other night or at least almost every other night, the energies and the voices in my head were gone almost immediately after the conversation ended. I had grown to expect them. Also, if I didn't write the information down, it would be quickly forgotten shortly after the conversation too. During an earlier "download," Archangel Michael explained it was the variation in my energy during and outside of the conversations. As soon as the conversations ended, my vibration returned to its normal level, and I could no longer recall the information shared because it was at a higher vibration. I wish I could say I understood, but I didn't, and I wouldn't for years to come.

I continued to have these conversations almost nightly, each time writing down as much as I could before forgetting most of what was shared with me. But I began to notice that I was reminded of the information or the concepts in unexpected ways. Sometimes it was books, other times it was an article or in advertisements. No matter what the impetus, the information came flooding back.

Let me share an example. I was flying a four-day trip right after one of the nights I just described. It had been a fairly long day and normally I'd head to my hotel room and call it a day. After all, I'd been awake for sixteen hours and had a twelve-hour flying day. That night, I was feeling restless and decided to go for a walk. It was a warm night in Boston, and the sidewalks were still quite full. Normally, I would have taken a right as I came out of the hotel and walked towards the river. It was just before dusk, and I loved to watch the rowing team on the river. This night, I chose to go left.

It was about 8:00 p.m. and off in the distance I could see the glow of the stadium lights and the faint roar of a crowd. *The Red Sox must be in town*, I thought, and I started to walk towards Fenway Park. I was enjoying the night air and the large numbers of families out for an evening stroll. Unfortunately, it was difficult to maintain a decent pace with the crowded sidewalk, so I decided to duck into the Barnes & Noble store. It would be closing in about forty-five minutes, and I figured I could browse for a while and then head back to the hotel.

My favorite sections have always been psychology and self-help. I made my way back to that corner of the store where I knew those sections were normally located. The store was surprisingly empty; in fact, the only people I noticed were sitting at the little coffee bar connected to the bookstore. As I strolled along, I glanced at the technology magazines stacked on the table adjacent to one of the aisles. Nothing there of interest.

Suddenly I heard a book hit the floor behind me. I turned around expecting to see someone, yet no one was there, but there on the floor was a book. I walked over and picked it up. The name of the book was *The Biology of Belief* written by Bruce Lipton. As I read a little more on the front and back covers, I became aware of the synchronicity of it falling to the floor. On the front, the subtitle read *Unleashing the Power of Consciousness, Matter & Miracles*. I flipped it over to read the back, "Stunning new scientific discoveries about the biochemical effects of the brain's functioning show that all cells of your body are affected by your thoughts." I made a mental note to read this book sometime and reached to put it back on the end cap. But it was completely full, and this specific book wasn't even displayed there. I looked at the shelves on each side of the rack. *The Biology of Belief* was nowhere to be found.

I had been getting better at understanding and believing that we are consciously getting messages to guide us on this journey. This was definitely one. Mary and I had moved to California several months prior, and this book was going back with me. It was written by one of the first scientists to recognize the commonalities and similarities in science and spirituality.

After purchasing my new friend, I was ready to venture back to the hotel. The number of people out on their evening strolls had decreased significantly, and I was able to make good time. There was a light fog moving into the city that added to the mysticism of the evening.

As I climbed into bed, I justified reading a few pages out of my new book to help me get to sleep. Two hours later, I finally closed it because I needed to get some sleep, not because I was ready to stop reading.

I loved the context of the book and completely resonated with what Dr. Lipton shared. But my biggest takeaway was that there are many discoveries outside the common science that we learn in school that have great relevance and significance in our lives. And then as if this thought was a switch, I started to remember: The guides shared with me that many things are predicated on our time and place of birth. They told me we chose our parents and their beliefs. Every circumstance in our life was created to help us on a journey we chose. The more I remembered, the more questions I had. I couldn't wait to get back to sleep. Maybe they would come again and bring more synchronicities.

Moment of Reflection

We have a tendency to believe that only the chosen few can get messages. The truth is, just like everything else, our beliefs affect our ability. If we are willing to listen and take action or guidance, it becomes easier and easier to get the messages. We learn to connect to the guidance. We learn to do it on a regular basis. The more comfortable we become, the more fluid the information. Like everything else, this takes time.

The more I connected, the more information I got. The more I took action, the more I trusted the message. The guidance was real, and I was learning it was helping me in understanding myself and my life. I was learning to trust the information. And with that trust, I was getting more specific information and making greater strides.

I loved getting the information, and I knew how important it would be to the work Mary and I were being called towards. I just didn't know how long I could physically survive this rigorous schedule created by these downloads.

Chapter Nineteen

Tapping In

*There is a vast amount of knowledge available
to you. All you have to do is ask and pay
attention. Every thought ever thought, any idea
anyone has had, and anything you could ever
imagine possible is available to you. The keys to
tapping into this knowledge are awareness and
vibration.*

The Round Table, channeled by Vince Kramer

Think of the popular phrase: Master your mind. It is how we truly can discover, create, and live the life we are meant to live. If we don't master our mind, we are truly living on autopilot. Our mind is defined as what we hold in our consciousness in that given moment. This means our mind changes with the level of consciousness we choose.

When we share the concept of mastering the mind, we are talking about being aware in the present moment. It is about being aware of the vibration and the level of consciousness a person is operating from. It is about being aware of thoughts and choosing ones that support. It is knowing the ego sub-personalities and when they are triggered. It is about learning how to work with these sub-personalities instead of opposing them. It is about being aware of all aspects of our being.

As I studied more and more about energy, I found how helpful an understanding of the concepts of quantum physics is. For example, two of the concepts can be extremely beneficial in understanding the reasons we must master our minds: We create our own reality, and we do it with our thoughts and feelings. Because our thoughts and feelings are energy, they have a vibration. To create, these thoughts and feelings must be in alignment with each other and in alignment with what we want to create. When we master our minds, we can stop thoughts that aren't in alignment and choose ones that are.

There are many ways that can help us on the journey to being the masters of our minds. Some of them are around understanding and becoming proficient in creating on purpose. Three of the most important are imagination, intent, and allowing. Other ways that we can effectively move towards mastery are working with our belief systems and integrating our personalities and sub-personalities in support of us living on purpose.

It all starts with learning to be aware of what is going on in our minds and our thoughts and being able to recognize when our mind is running away from us. It is about quieting it long enough to stop the automatic thinking and reactions. There are so many ways to do this, I stumbled on one that worked for me.

After another night of waking up to information coming in, I knew I wouldn't get back to sleep. Mary had suggested over several weeks that I ask Michael and the gang to slow it down or limit the downloads to a couple nights during the week. I was concerned and hesitant at the same time. I was afraid that if I asked them to slow down, the information would stop coming all together or I'd miss out on something I might need to know. I wanted all of this information and I knew I was meant to share it. But I did need to get my sleep if I was going to put together the materials in a way that people would accept and, most importantly, would be willing to implement in their daily lives. It was a true dilemma for me, but I was not willing to slow down the flow just because I was tired. I'd have to learn how to not let it affect Mary or my day job.

At the time, Mary and I had moved from Redondo Beach to Torrance, California. We liked the new place especially because we had doubled our living space. Although it was a little farther away from the water, it was worth it. We had moved to California to be close to the beach, the warm weather, and the amenities that were so much nicer and more accessible. The one thing that was missing was a place for us to stretch and move our bodies.

We had doubled the living area, but we still had just over one thousand square feet. We needed to find someplace to work out. I'd been experiencing a lot of joint pain from old sports injuries, and it seemed like from the late-night experiences with the downloads from the Masters. Mary suggested that we try yoga. With all the pain that I was experiencing, I was ready to try just about anything.

Mary picked up her laptop and moved outside to be among the roses as she started her research. She loves to be in beauty, and it always proves more productive. A quick search of Google led us to a yoga studio fairly close—walking distance—from our new condo. It had a funny name, Dahn Yoga, but the proximity just couldn't be ignored. We decided we would visit the very next day.

As we walked the six blocks to the studio, we took in the wonder of Southern California. We enjoyed the gentle breeze generated by the ocean and the sounds of the swaying palm trees. The sun was just rising in the east and the warmth on our backs was a pleasing contrast to the cool breeze on our faces. I started to wonder if this was the right move or the right place. I expressed my concerns about the yogis we might meet and why the studio had such a funny name. At 6'5" and 240 pounds, I wasn't what one would consider graceful, and I felt self-conscious when classes were too advanced. Mary, in a great act of kindness, ensured me I'd be fine.

When we arrived at the studio, it was easy to see that this wasn't a normal yoga studio, and we soon would learn it wasn't normal yoga. The front of the studio, what I would consider the storefront, was small with a few chairs strategically placed around the room mostly because there wasn't much room for them. Oddly, there wasn't a sales counter or check in desk. The decor was all Asian with pictures of a distinguished Asian gentleman, news clippings that also included this person, and schedules lining the walls. There were two doors opposite the glass door we entered. Both of them, completely solid with no windows, were closed. There were no placards on them so we were left to trying to guess what might be behind each of them.

Almost immediately, a tall, thin woman appeared from the door on the right. Her long black hair contrasted her white karate-type attire. She was obviously quite fit, but not the yoga teacher one would expect. She introduced herself as Jin-Ae. Although she was a very beautiful woman, it was her energy that was so captivating. She was calm, collected, and unguarded. Her presence alone made us want to be part of what was happening at this studio. Her energy made us feel loved and accepted. We were going to buy before she said anything other than hello.

Jin invited us to sit and explained the concept of Dahn Yoga, which is a Korean physical exercise system founded by Ilchi Lee. It was Ilchi Lee whose pictures decorated the walls of the room. She shared that the practice of Dahn Yoga has three major components: mastery of the mind, the use of energy to enhance the brain-body connection, and self-managed holistic care. She continued to share the premises of their teachings.

Sometimes things in life make us feel uneasy and very uncomfortable. What she shared was one of those things for me. I was squirming in my chair like a toddler that has been asked to sit in one place for more than a few minutes. I kept looking at Mary to get her reaction. I guess I wanted her to show she was as uncomfortable as I was. I didn't want to be there, yet I knew it was exactly where I was *supposed* to be. Before we left, we were signed up for three months and were the proud owners of our own karate-looking uniforms. Quite different from the stylish yoga clothes often seen at other yoga studios.

The first three months were amazing. I was challenged by the unfamiliar and specific exercises aimed specifically at energy—both to increase and to move it in the body—and mastery of the mind. In addition to the expected relief from pain and stiffness, Dahn Yoga improved my overall health: I lost weight, felt much better, and my mind was clearer. Because Mary felt the same way, we signed up for the following year.

Little did I know this was all leading up to something extremely powerful in this awakening journey I'd been on. I couldn't see it at the time, but every success was helping me trust what was to come.

One of my favorite parts of the program helped in mastering my mind. I had to find the discipline to hold yoga poses for long periods of time. The burn of muscles, the voices in my head, and the desire to just quit all worked against my inner will. I had to dig deep and choose not to quit. We all need to learn just how powerful our mind is, but also how fast the wrong thoughts can sabotage us.

I learned a lot about mind and body control in my time practicing Dahn Yoga. From that very first day, Mary and I knew there was a specific reason we picked that place. It became relatively obvious quickly. In holding poses like sleeping tiger for over forty-five minutes, it was clear that we could master the mind and we would learn the importance in understanding that in our work in the future. I have to admit, it was so gratifying to feel the resistance of my body through the aching muscles and find the peacefulness in my mind. Becoming one with thoughts and overcoming great pain can be rewarding and helpful in life's challenges.

I actually learned to control the wandering mind. The unnecessary or unwanted thoughts were fewer and further between. I learned to trust myself and understand that my thoughts were my choice. I remember specifically one afternoon when I wanted to nap before a late evening flight, my mind went on a tear. I was thinking about everything and anything. Any time I got close to sleep, something else would pop into my mind. I decided in that moment to choose to let these thoughts in, or not. I decided I would not let them come from autopilot. And I fell asleep immediately. I realized I was in charge. I was the master of my mind and body.

My absolute favorite part of the Dahn Yoga experience was the magnet meditations. We used special magnets to become aware of their energy and then notice and connect with our personal energy. I didn't know it at the time, but it prepared me to channel at the level I do. I knew at that point that we are all energy and there is energy all around us. I wasn't aware of this energy in the past because I couldn't quiet my mind long enough to experience it or work with it. I remember the day I had my breakthrough during a magnet meditation. It was life changing.

As I was sitting cross legged on the floor, I followed the suggestion of Jin as she led us into the experience. Before we started at Dahn Yoga, I had heard of chakras and dabbled in feeling the energy in them. Since joining, I had learned to feel and move the energy even more in these centers. Once again, something so far from my beliefs was blowing me away and opening me to a world of possibility that I couldn't have ever imagined even just a few months earlier. Everything had been happening so fast because I made the decision to be open and willing to try everything then choosing only what is right for me.

I vividly remember the very meditation that truly was a quantum leap in my life. It was a real transformation. We started the meditation just like every other one, sitting and using magnets to facilitate the flow of energy. I felt the energy building more rapidly than any time before. It started out with a tingling in each center, and then moved to a swirl. I felt the energy move out from my body. Jin shared that by moving the magnet up the body to certain places, we could create a higher vibration at each of these centers.

We started at the lower chakra or energy center and made our way to each center until we reached the center at the top of our heads. My body was vibrating chaotically yet, I was relaxed, calm, and felt in alignment.

Jin asked us to put our magnets down and feel the energy. I put my attention on and felt each area that she identified as an energy center. I felt it swirling and I felt real power in it. When I got to the top of my head, it still felt like we were using the magnet. I had that dizzy feeling of standing up too fast. And then it happened; I saw the colors that I normally see in the middle of the night. This had never happened before. I had never been awake and brought in the colors before. I had always been awakened to them. I concentrated on a different Master and the color changed. I concentrated and tunneled my vision into seeing the color begin to swirl just like I felt the energy centers do with the magnet. It felt like my body temperature had risen ten degrees. My body started to shake like it did that day in Vancouver, but I was not panicked like I was then. I had felt it before, and I knew what was happening. I was opening to yet another level of accepting this energy. It was another step on this journey that had started five years earlier.

I mentally asked a question, and I heard a familiar voice. Then, in my mind's eye, I saw the blue energy of Archangel Michael. It was swirling and the connection was stronger than I have ever had. It was amazing. I brought in the energy myself for the very first time. *What does this mean?* I started to think about it and analyze it. And it was gone just as fast as it came. I was disappointed I lost it, but I couldn't wait to tell Mary. It was so exciting; I felt like a little boy that just rode his two-wheeler for the first time. I felt like a big boy.

As we got in the car after our class together, I looked over at Mary excitedly. She was in her Dahn Yoga uniform just like I was. We wore baggy blue ankle-cuffed pants with baggy short-sleeved white shirts. Every time I looked at Mary in her baggy uniform it made me smile inside. I looked just as goofy, but we both knew the theory behind the clothing was to allow the energy we'd generate in class to flow. She had her flip flops on and had one leg pulled underneath her with the window down. We both loved how we felt after class.

I was so eager to share that I had heard a voice! "Mary, I heard a voice in our meditation!"

She snapped her head to look at me with a huge smile on her face. "You are kidding! I haven't been able to see any colors of the energy and now you are hearing voices?" She was excited for me but at the same time frustrated. "It figures that you would not only see colors but then hear a voice. I'm jealous!"

I'm not sure why I could get out of the way and let the energy flow. Maybe, it was because I had learned to compartmentalize so well as a pilot. "It will happen for you. I know it will," I tried to assure her.

"How did it go?" she asked.

"It was different from my experiences at night," I explained. "I was only able to hear a few words."

She urged me to tell her more, "What did you ask?"

"I asked if the blue energy I was seeing was Archangel Michael," I answered.

"What did you hear?" she wanted to know.

"It is I," I shared the only words I heard. There was nothing else to tell her because it came and went so fast. "That was it, there was nothing more."

"This is fantastic, Vince! You have to keep meditating like this. It is amazing how you can see and feel the energies. Wow, what a breakthrough!"

We both were silent for the remainder of the short drive home. I could still feel the energy in my body. I wasn't sure what this all meant or where it was going. But the energy felt amazing, and I didn't want to miss a second of feeling it.

This meditation led to many more just like it. I was able to move into that space, work with the energy, and bring in the four guides that had been working with me the last five years. It was a monumental quantum leap. I knew. I no longer had to wait for the Masters to appear. I could move into a space where I could call them in and then connect with the energy. It became clear that understanding energy was essential for everyone.

Moment of Reflection

We are all energy. In fact, everything is energy. All energy can react and interact with any other energy. Thoughts are energy and feelings are energy. Even ideas are energy. The Universe is all one energy, and we are part of that one energy. Which means we can tap into any thought that has been thought. We can tap into any idea that someone has ever had. We are privy to the divine knowledge of the entire universe. We have access to every possibility. It isn't for a chosen few. It is for me, and it is for everyone. We just need to know how to tap into and take action.

Chapter Twenty
Getting Out of the Way

Your gifts are meant to be shared in the world.
To fully live your life in alignment with purpose,
you will use all your gifts in your interactions
with others.

The Round Table, channeled by Vince Kramer

It is one thing to be open to believing that guidance is being given to us in many different ways, yet it is something completely different to believe that each person can allow the guidance to come through them. I didn't necessarily *want* to bring in guidance because I was afraid of what information would come through. I was afraid I might influence the information, and I definitely didn't want anyone to judge me. After all of those fears, I just wasn't sure what to expect and how it would affect my body, which are all the reasons I consistently rejected Mary's urgings of trying to channel those who continued to visit me at night.

I now know we all have the capability to connect to this guidance. And we all do it in different ways. Some connect to the energy and are able to share it in their writing. Others get the information and share it in discussions. Still others share the guidance in the things in life that they are good at or enjoy doing. Many movies are written, directed and/or produced with the help of channeled guidance. People share that they didn't know where the inspiration came from; it was just there.

Many authors have shared that they sat down to write, and the words just flowed through them. That is channeling guidance. We all have the capability to tap into this guidance, our guidance. We just have to learn to move beyond the stigma and learn how to trust. We must learn to allow ourselves to be open, accepting, and allowing.

From my experiences and interactions with others, I no longer have the fears I mentioned earlier. One thing that has changed along the way is the way I have experienced the energy in my body when working with higher vibrations. When I connect and bring in those vibrations, it is the most amazing feeling. Others have shared that they have identical expressions of the vibrations.

The most intense feeling is the deepest expression of love coursing through my body. My entire body is enveloped in a warmth that is impossible to explain. But it wasn't always that way, it started out quite differently. Let me explain.

I had experienced four nights in a row of being awakened with messages. I loved getting the information that was being shared with me. I knew all of it would be part of the programs and trainings I've been called to share since I told my grandma about what I wanted to do all those years ago. But this had to stop. I couldn't take much more of the lack of sleep. I wanted the information, but I couldn't and wouldn't fly tired for my safety and the safety of my crew and passengers.

It was only 4:00 a.m. and my eyes were heavy again as I looked over at Mary. I was tired and wanted to go back to sleep, but my thoughts were even heavier, and they kept me awake. My brain was wide awake, and my body was exhausted. There had to be another way. I owed it to myself. I owed it to Mary. I owed it to my passengers to be rested. But I knew that I must get this information because I'm meant to share it with the world. I lie there waiting for Mary to open her eyes.

Thank goodness we were going to Dahn Yoga every day that I wasn't flying. It recharged my batteries, and I realized I was at a higher vibration or frequency after every session. Life flowed much easier the days we went. My favorite days were still meditation days. I was able to bring the colors into my mind much easier now and I was able to connect to my four guides and hear their information just like at night when they came in. That day's meditation was extra strong, and I didn't want to leave it. I normally just saw the blue, green, red, and gold colors dance in my inner vision as I heard the different messages. Lately, I had been seeing different colors, like orange, purple, white, and magenta to name a few. It was exciting and concerning at the same time. It all made me wonder at times if I was just making it up.

I was able to fall asleep for a few more hours of much-needed sleep.

I woke up to the smell of breakfast and made my way to the kitchen.

"Good morning," Mary said cheerfully.

"Good morning," I repeated.

In a hurried voice Mary suggested, "Go get dressed for yoga, I made us breakfast sandwiches for the walk to the studio." Within minutes, we were on our way.

During the meditation that day, I heard words about choosing our parents so we can experience life in our own unique way. That statement still felt out of alignment with my beliefs at the time. There was no way I made that up. Maybe that is why I wanted to stay in meditation, I felt connected. It all made more sense when I was deep into the experience and not affected by the outside world. It no longer mattered who was leading the meditation. We had a visiting instructor one day because our usual instructor on Thursdays, Chinally, was providing free body energy readings at a local store. My energy during the meditation was so powerful and profound that both Mary and I wondered what to do with it. She suggested we go see Chinally, hoping the walk would ground me.

After class, we said our ceremonial thank yous and goodbyes. We asked our visiting instructor where we could find Chinally. He gave us the specific store where she was giving the readings and we were out the door.

"You might even get an energy reading while you are there," he hollered out as we walked out the door. The message didn't have to be any clearer. We were meant to go and get a reading. Mary and I had had readings before and agreed it might be fun to confirm the high vibration of our energy after a session of yoga and a powerful connection during meditation.

Chinally was set up in a local grocery store of all places. As soon as we walked through the sliding doors and shared pleasantries with the greeter, we spied her at a table near the entry to the fresh produce. She was radiant as always, and the bright colors of the fruit behind her paled in comparison. She was only 5'3" but her presence was huge. She was joined by another lady that we had seen at the studio several times. They were both standing behind a table that had a banner stretched across the front with the company logo in the top left corner and the name and tagline proudly displayed across the banner. There was a single chair on the left side of the table. We noticed that there was a lady in her fifties sitting in the chair and a small line consisting of one man and two ladies off to the side waiting their turn. In front of the table looking through the many pamphlets was a girl in her twenties. Chinally's endeavor seemed to be a big success with all this interest. And it was a very diverse group of people.

As we approached the table, we could see that the lady in the chair had her hand on a pad. We had had energy readings before and knew that there was a metal handprint on the pad that is a sensor to pick up the electromagnetic energy being emitted from her body. There was also a camera that took a picture of the person sitting in the chair. The pad and camera were connected to a computer that Chinally was operating. The computer program took the electromagnetic inputs and the photo from the camera and created a picture of the image surrounded by the energetic aura representation. There was a third device hard wired to the computer. It was a printer to provide an actual photo of the picture on the computer screen. It was a very similar set up to others we had seen.

When Chinally saw us, she lit up like the sun. She greeted us with the same Korean greeting we learned at the yoga center and motioned for us to get in line. She had such a big heart that made people want to please her. It was like wanting to be worthy of the love she shared with those around her.

We came straight from working out and we were still in our uniforms. We were getting just as much attention as the banner on the table. I'm sure Chinally was happy we came in because we were practically a walking billboard for her business. At this point, there were five more people in line behind us and three people standing at the table asking questions about the center and the programs they offer. We shared our experiences with the others in line. It felt good to share and we knew it was a precursor of things to come for us.

It was finally our turn and Mary went first. She sat down in the chair and placed her hand on the silver hand on the receptor pad. Chinally asked her to smile and clicked her picture. She only had to hold her hand there for about a minute as Chinally's assistant typed away on the computer's keyboard. After a few more clicks, Mary's image showed up on the screen. There was a brilliant full yellow aura surrounding her. There was also a bright green patch of light over her heart. Some more clicks on the computer and the assistant started printing the image on the screen. A few short minutes later, the photo emerged from the printer. Chinally grabbed the picture and motioned for Mary to join her behind the table. She was very animated and her excitement to share the results with Mary was quite contagious. She was like a little kid bubbling over with joy.

It was my turn. As I sat down, I couldn't help but remember the very first time I got a similar reading. I questioned the validity and accuracy of what seemed like a pretty basic way of measuring energy. But I must admit, the reading was so accurate that I couldn't deny the results or the explanation of them. That reading was given to me by a complete stranger, and I was looking forward to hearing what Chinally would have to share.

I placed my hand on the pad, click, click, and another click, and the printer came to life. I was finished. When in the chair, the image on the computer screen is out of view. As soon as I got the chance, I stood up and peeked around the edge of the computer to see the image on the screen. I was shocked at what I saw. It had been almost two years since I had a reading, and I'd changed a lot. In past readings, I had never seen anything even close to this. The entire screen was filled with color. My image was surrounded with a large white arc of light. Segmenting the white arc, almost in half, was a band of medium blue. In each upper corner of the screen was a deep scarlet patch of energy. Across my chest were patches of medium blue, yellow, and green from my left to right. Chinally already had the photo in her hand when I looked up and she was excitedly waving me over towards her.

When I got over to her, she had a very serious look on her face. I am not sure I had ever seen her without a smile. I felt myself getting very nervous and I bit down on my lip. *Is there something wrong?* She was just staring at the picture and continued to stare at it for several moments without saying a word. I was freaked as I began to rock the entire weight of my body foot to foot in anticipation of some bad news.

She finally spoke without taking her eyes off the photo. "Who *are* you?" She asked.

I was confused, but by the tone of her voice, she was perplexed and amazed at the same time by what she saw.

"You are a teacher, and I should be learning from you," she said sincerely as she stared deep into my eyes.

I believed she was looking into my heart. At least it felt like she was seeing that far into me.

I didn't know what to say and finally managed to blurt out a shy "Thank you."

I knew she was seeing the energy that I had connected with in my meditation as well as the vibrational frequencies of my night visits. Her acknowledgment was the confirmation I needed.

By that time, there were ten people in line for a reading. It seemed that our energy tended to attract people. Mary and I decided we should move on and allow others to have their time. After all, this was to introduce people to Dahn Yoga and bring new members into the center.

We talked about our readings all the way home. Energetically, we had been expanding with the help of each other, our yoga experience, and the visits by the Masters. Life had been a whirlwind and we both received verification. We are here to bring the information I am getting to the world, and we are meant to do it together. We agreed to continue our conversation later when we had fewer distractions.

Although it was a difficult decision, I realized our move to a fifty-five and older community was a smart one. Literally a week after we decided we needed more space, I turned fifty-five and an amazing opportunity fell in our laps. This was a perfect place for us to do the work on ourselves that we had been asked to do. We thought we made the choice, but it seemed like the Universe made available exactly what we needed.

As I stepped through our sliding doors out onto the patio, I was glad we moved from the traffic noise of the beach cities. I missed the sounds, sights, and smells of the ocean, but this move afforded us the quiet atmosphere to make some big decisions in moving forward and in understanding why we were together and how we were going to share it with the world.

Mary was already out on the patio sitting in one of our two beach chairs. As I joined her, I couldn't help but notice the gentle breeze blowing through the palm trees as they swayed in unison. It was the perfect setting on the perfect day to have the conversation we were about to engage in.

As I settled into my chair, Mary began the conversation. "I know we have talked about this before, but we need to do something about you being awake so much at night." She continued, "Hear me out before you say anything."

I had heard this statement or request before, and I knew we were going to talk about something that had been a challenging topic of conversation in the past. She wasted no time in getting right to the point, "I think you should consider channeling. Your reading with Chinally earlier today and what is happening to you during the meditations are proof. I know you can do it. And if you will let the information come through in a channeling, then maybe you could sleep through the night."

We had talked about this all before, and I wasn't very receptive.

Truthfully, I must admit that the thought scared me. As Mary shared this, the reasons I shouldn't or couldn't channel came flooding into my head. My ego was engaged big time. Several voices shared all at the same time why it wasn't a good idea. They were a chaotic chorus of doubt and fear. I was worried that I might not be able to do it. I was worried I might make things up. I was worried I might affect or change something that was shared by the guides and mess up someone's life. Basically, I was worried.

I didn't feel comfortable, capable, and most of all, I didn't feel worthy.

But then again, Mary made sense. I was able to connect even more easily because of the nightly visits. I could hear them loud and clear in my meditations. Maybe I *should* try. It would be nice to sleep through the night. It would also be nice for Mary to hear the information first-hand instead of filtered through me. I didn't know how I would ever go about it, yet another tug of war going on in my head. It was so loud I didn't even hear Mary who was continuing to try and convince me it was a good idea. Her voice just blended with the ones in my head.

I closed my eyes just for a second. And in that second, I agreed to try.

I couldn't believe I said it, but I did, and Mary heard it. I said it, and I was sure she wouldn't forget I did. Then the question was *How would I go about it?* My brain shifted into overdrive, and I began to think of ways that I could get out of the way enough for a channeling to even be possible. And then it hit me just like a 2x4 against my head. Mary and I were certified in hypnosis. Maybe she could take me into a deep theta brain state and that would work. I shared my idea with her. She had been asking me to try for many months to do this. She was immediately on board.

"Let's do it right now," she exclaimed.

"NO," I refused. "We can do it tomorrow afternoon."

It took me about twenty minutes to agree to exactly when I would do it the next day. I finally had an agreement with her and the voices in my head calmed down. I knew they would be back because Mary wouldn't let me forget that we agreed on it the very next day. She couldn't wait for me to be ready and because I said yes, she wouldn't let me change my mind.

Mary was like a child waiting for Christmas morning. It would truly be a gift for her if I could channel the Masters and the angels. The anticipation of finding out seemed too much for her

The next morning after another night of messages, as soon as I opened my eyes, she asked if I'd be ready to try. I reminded her I said in the afternoon, and she reluctantly stopped asking. After lunch, I couldn't hold her back any longer and I agreed. It was as if I had agreed to buy her a new house. She was ecstatic and more than ready. She was actually giggling like I imagined she did as a little girl growing up in Northern California. I, on the other hand, was extremely apprehensive, but I chose to surrender to my decision and to try.

Mary set up a beautiful space and played some meditation music. It helped me relax although not completely. It felt much like I was meeting a girl's parents before a first date. How could I ever live up to the expectations? I closed my eyes and listened to the music. It allowed me to settle into a more receptive place. When I didn't feel the pressure of "making" this all happen, I lay down on the floor and let Mary know I was ready.

She kneeled next to me and started talking me through the process of relaxing my body from my feet up to the top of my head. I felt the tension leaving as each part of my body relaxed. The anxiety of trying something new and being able to perform was gone. We used the technique of moving in my mind to a safe space that we built when we were learning hypnosis. Mary expertly guided me into that space.

My eyes were closed, but I sensed she was smiling at me. She had wanted me to channel for so long. She said to me in a hypnotic voice, "Okay, relax and try to let your mind go blank. You are good at this."

Just her voice took away some of the self-induced anxiety of letting these energies talk through me. I don't think I was scared. I had seen others do it many times. I just didn't know what to expect, how I would feel.

"Breathe slowly in and out, and let your muscles relax one by one. As you continue to breathe, let's start at your feet. Put your focus on your feet, breathe and relax," she continued.

I had learned to self-hypnotize at a younger age, and I found it easy to relax my feet and ankles at her suggestion.

Mary went on, "Now focus on your lower legs, thighs, and hip area."

The anxiety was leaving my body. The self-hypnosis training was helping greatly.

In a soft steady tone Mary suggested, "Keep breathing slowly and deeply as you move your focus up to your stomach, chest, and shoulders. Keep breathing in and out and feel your arms and hands relax. Take another deep breath as you relax your face, back of your neck, and top of your head. You are doing great."

With that reassurance I felt my body completely relax as I moved fully into a theta brain wave state.

"Now, allow your body to stay in this relaxed place as you move into your own personal space. Perfect, you are doing well."

My personal space is a red rock outcropping in the middle of a wooded area. There is a stone path that parallels a meandering creek that leads to this outcropping. There are many animals that call this wooded area home and usually show up when I enter it. At the top of the outcropping are two areas that form natural lounge-type seats in the rocks facing each other. It took no time at all to see myself comfortably in one of the seats, relaxed and open to this new experience.

While I was deeply relaxed and moving on my own towards my sacred space and saw myself take a seat, I could still hear Mary's gentle voice suggesting that I call in the guides. I know she continued talking to me, but I never heard her. I knew I was in the room, but at the same time I felt separate from it.

I used the technique I learned in my Dahn Yoga meditations to call in the guides. Suddenly, I saw the color blue moving like a kaleidoscope in my head. It was mesmerizing and almost hypnotic. I don't know exactly how to explain what happened next, other than to say I heard the word *hello* in my head for several seconds and felt the need for it to come out of my mouth. It was like the word itself was too much and I began to cough and hack. It was like the energy of the word was more than my body could handle. After several minutes, I heard the word *hello* come out of my mouth. That was the last that I remembered until I opened my eyes sometime later. The whole experience seemed to be about five minutes. I physically felt very well except for my eyes feeling full of energy and very tired.

As I felt myself become aware of my body, I felt relaxed and at peace. I started to open my eyes and I heard Mary's voice.

She was so excited as she exclaimed, "Vince, that was amazing! You did it! You channeled!" Mary's enthusiasm filled my completely relaxed body with excitement and warmth.

She continued, "I'm sure the guides knew I was pretty blown away by this, so they did most of the talking. I wouldn't have known what to do or say anyway! But the feeling was amazing, and it is so exciting to have this connection with them!"

I felt somewhat relieved. And I was tired. Although I could still barely focus my eyes, I could see Mary looking like a little kid on Christmas day.

And she asked enthusiastically, "When can we do it again??"

Mary shared that I had channeled Archangel Michael and the channeling lasted for over forty minutes. I couldn't believe it was that long and when I glanced up at the clock, sure enough, it had been almost an hour since I lay down on the floor. I don't remember anything other than the initial hellos. I asked Mary what happened. She filled me in on the conversation she had from the notes she took.

She assured me that everything went fine and there was nothing said that I should have concern over. It was basically all about my willingness to channel the energies and the willingness of the energies to come through me in this manner. Mary had recorded the forty minutes and I was able to listen to the experience. It was hard to accept that it actually happened because I had no memory of it. Like my first channeling with Eloryia, it felt very strange and I'm not sure I believed it fully. I can't explain what happened or what was said. What I do know is I felt different than I had felt before. I was calm and more open to accepting that there may be things I wouldn't understand but that didn't mean something didn't happen. I had actually heard it in the recording. There was an ease going on inside me, and I felt extremely good physically. At that moment, I knew I would do it again with more confidence and with less doubt.

All of a sudden, I succumbed to tiredness, and I fell asleep right there on the floor. I slept for almost an hour. It was one of the most restful naps I had ever experienced.

Moment of Reflection

We all have the ability to connect into this guidance or what I would call divine knowledge. But because it has been considered taboo or wrong in the past, over time, the human race lost contact.

When we are willing to accept that we are basically tapping into a higher frequency of the exact same energy that we are, we can realize that this is more a birthright than a woo woo concept only for the few. In connecting with the highest vibrations of our energy streams, we open to the unlimited possibilities that are available when we choose.

Chapter Twenty-One

Voices in My Head

The resistance that you feel is from the inside.
Many times in your life, you have experienced
self-sabotage, designed to keep you safe. The
parts of you are real. You must get to know them
and integrate them into your team. They will
always be in the way until they learn to trust
you.

The Round Table, channeled by Vince Kramer

When we were born, we needed a way that we could interact with other people. Just like a computer, we needed an operating system. Our operating system is our ego or our personality. It is the way that we feel, think, and act in life and interacting with others. We begin forming our personality before birth and continue throughout our lives. The characteristics of our personality are inherent and acquired.

The inherent characteristics come from our perceptions and judgments of what we experience. We experience the circumstances in our lives and give them meaning. We form beliefs around these meanings and choose how to act based on these beliefs. Over time, these beliefs become a habit. Habits become patterns. Patterns become behavior. And, just like that, our operating system has been formed.

There are times in our life where our main personality isn't equipped to handle a circumstance that happens. When this happens, we develop a sub-personality or alter ego to deal with the situation. The majority of the circumstances that result in a sub-personality being formed are based in tragedy or trauma. These sub-personalities are developed to keep us safe. The circumstances that led up to the tragedy or trauma are triggers for these personalities. Words, actions, even smells can awaken the sub-personality that will take charge in that moment.

Because these sub-personalities were formed to keep us safe, they will do anything to keep us from moving forward. They would rather have us be safe than happy. They would rather have us stuck than successful. They never grow older. If formed at seven, that part of the sub-personality will always act like a seven-year-old.

The sub-personality is experienced in many different ways. One of the most common ways is a voice in the head. Sometimes those voices sound like mother or father. No matter what that voice sounds like, it will do anything to keep a person safe which means it is keeping them from moving forward.

Like most, I have experienced these voices. They have shown up throughout the process of awakening to bring science and spirituality together to live my unique purpose.

The morning after I agreed to channel for Mary for the first time, there was a plethora of extremely active voices in my head. At least thanks to the nightly downloads, I knew the voices weren't my guides, the Masters. They didn't sound like the Masters at all, and their messages were all negative. I had heard these voices before and I know now that they were sub-personalities that I had formed early in my life. The main jobs of these ego personalities were to keep me safe at times in my life when I didn't feel safe. I had formed them at an early age to protect myself from situations that I didn't know how to handle. Decades later, they were still trying to keep me safe even if it was no longer necessary.

In the years to come, I'd learn that I could have worked with them and quieted them. I could have eliminated the self-sabotage they created. But as I heard them at the time of the channeling with Mary, I was forced to listen because I didn't know any different. This wasn't the first time I'd heard these familiar voices. I had heard them many times before. One specific time was after I met Mary at Carlos' Bistro.

Let me explain what it was like. Think of a cartoon or a movie where they depict or describe someone that has an angel on one shoulder and a devil on the other. That is what it was like in my head that morning. One voice was telling me why I could and should trust Mary, and the other was telling why there is no way she could understand what I was going through and how it would be a complete waste of time talking to her.

It is normal to have these internal debates. What wasn't normal was the extra conversations that were going on in my head, all at the same time that morning. It seemed like there was a committee of five or more. There are two different voices that I have heard on a regular basis throughout my adult life. They have always shown up when I meet new people. Actually, they show up when I start to get to know someone a little better.

One voice is the one that wants me to not be alone. It is the angel on my shoulder. This voice is always encouraging me to get to know someone better. It is very trusting and always sees the best in that person. It is always encouraging me to make this person my new friend. This voice was especially strong that morning. It was telling me what a nice person Mary is and reminding me of the strange and overpowering attraction I had for her in Cabo. It pointed out how kind she was the night at the poker game and how she understood me and what I was sharing with her.

The other voice, I was also very familiar with. It was the voice that shows up every time I meet someone new and like them immediately. It is the voice of doubt that doesn't trust anyone. This voice is the devil in my metaphor. It believes that everyone is out for themselves and always has an ulterior motive. The voice wants me to make anyone and everyone prove themselves before I allow them into my life or let them get close.

Just like the angel and devil in the cartoons, the voices were competing in my head. Both were trying to be heard, both wanted to be right, and both wanted me to do it their way. As always, I was torn between the two, but this time was different. Normally when this war inside my head happened, I chose to follow the devil, that voice that wanted me to back off. I would make the person prove to me that they weren't going to hurt me and that I could trust them before I let them into my life. This time was different; I took charge and listened to the voice that wanted me to trust Mary. I listened to my heart instead of my head and I was already glad I did.

And then, five years later I heard the same voices, just a few hours after the channeling. I recognized them, but I wasn't sure what they wanted from me.

Mary had gone shopping and I was sitting outside on our deck with our pug, Baby Joe. It was late afternoon, and the sun was still very high in the sky and at the same time was reflecting off the Pacific Ocean up onto the deck. Baby Joe was catching an afternoon nap, so I closed my eyes too.

As soon as I did, I heard, "What are people going to think?" I knew immediately the voice I was hearing was one of my sub-personalities. I had done some research after learning about the sub-personalities during a nightly download and I recognized this voice as the Image Consultant. The Image Consultant, mine especially, wants to make sure that people see me in a certain way, and they don't judge me negatively.

"What are people going to think about you channeling?" I heard again. Over the next thirty to forty minutes, I heard a barrage of derogatory statements from several discernible voices in my head. Their statements were all based on beliefs that I had formed during a lifetime of structure and influence from the world around me. These beliefs came from my parents, teachers, religion, and society. Beliefs about good and evil, heaven and hell. Beliefs I had about right and wrong that had come from the beliefs of others. Beliefs I had accepted from others because they were older and knew better than me.

I was being bombarded with statements and reasons based on many beliefs of others that I just accepted without thought or reasoning. It continued with the Image Consultant also being joined by my Protector and Critic, two sub-personalities that we all have.

The voice that I recognized as my Image Consultant was worried about how I might be seen by others and that I wouldn't be accepted by my family or friends. It said that channeling wasn't acceptable for a professional man or an airline pilot. It was adamant and persistent in sharing all the reasons why channeling, and more importantly why I, wouldn't be accepted or believed. What others would think and what they would say was pointed out by this voice over and over again.

The voice that I had learned was my Critic, was there to point out why and how I was wrong in believing that I could or deserved to channel. Who did I think I was to deserve to talk to angels or Masters? Why did I think that these energies would or should come to me? Did I think I was better than everyone else? Did I think I was special for some specific reason? The Critic continued to ask question after question and point out reason after reason of why I couldn't and didn't deserve to do this impossible thing called *channeling*. It wanted to be sure that I knew there was something wrong with me if I believed in it and especially if I believed that I could do it.

The third voice that I heard that day very distinctly was the one I know now as my Protector. The Protector's main job is just as the name implies. It was formed to protect me from being hurt or hurting myself. The Protector was confused on why I would want to bring that type of attention to myself. Didn't I know that people would judge me? I was a pilot and people would think I'd become unstable. I could lose my job. It pointed out that my parents wouldn't accept me, channeling was against my religion, and people wouldn't want to be around me. The list went on and on. The Protector did not want me to hurt myself or let anyone else hurt me over something so absurd.

I sat there in the sun for what seemed like hours as I was bombarded by my sub-personalities. I already had doubts and was questioning channeling and my ability to do it. I was worried about what others might think. And as I had my beliefs used against me by these three parts of myself, I started to wonder if I made it all up and why. I knew I wouldn't be able to share any of this with my family. I didn't feel comfortable sharing it with friends and I still questioned whether it was contradictory or completely opposite of my religious beliefs. After twelve years of Catholic school, I had to wonder if this was completely against those beliefs or not.

Mary had shared with me time and time again that there are different ways of looking at things. As I contemplated those words, I remember back to the months after the divorce from Martha. I had lost myself along the way and I had promised myself that I would be open to new ideas and possibilities. I agreed to try new things and hold on to the things that felt right. My connection to these higher vibrational energies felt right. I knew I had to continue this journey to discovering more.

In that moment, I chose to channel the energies, but I would only do it for Mary and family and friends that I knew would accept the channeling and me as a channel. The voices seem to accept that conscious choice, at least in that moment.

Moment of Reflection

We all have sub-personalities to protect us. We need to learn to identify them and learn to work with them. Many may have heard they have to get rid of the ego or move beyond it. Those personalities are and will always be a part of each of us. And we need to work with them.

The good news is that they were mostly formed when we were young. They were formed before the frontal lobe of the brain was fully developed. This was before we had reasoning capability. Now we can look at them from the adult brain and learn where we no longer need the protection of these sub-personalities.

I was able to learn how to work with these sub-personalities instead of fighting against them. As I felt safe and was willing to show my main personality not hidden by a mask or protected by an alter ego, I was free to show up in the world as my authentic self. As I learned to look at the negative parts of my past through adult eyes, I moved beyond staying small and was willing to step beyond the limits imposed by these sub-personalities. I was able to move forward at a faster pace supported by the sub-personalities that at one time held me back.

Chapter Twenty-Two

A Seat at The Table

*You all have gifts that you are meant to share
with others. Sharing them is important to
serving the world in the way that only you can.*

The Round Table, channeled by Vince Kramer

The more comfortable I got with channeling and receiving promptings, the more they came. And the more they came, the more comfortable I became with them. Over time my body adapted to the higher energetic vibrations of the channelings which allowed the guidance to come through more clearly and freely. I also learned to connect to the guidance through a form of self-hypnosis. I was able to connect on demand both in channeling for Mary and in downloading information on my own.

As I saw evidence of what was shared in the channelings, it was becoming easier and easier for me. I was able to connect to the Masters by using a technique that I learned in a book many years prior to even considering channeling. I was able to make the connection much faster. The coughing and hacking that happened as I made connection with the higher vibration was not as severe and lasted for much shorter time frames. I learned quickly that the vibrations affected my eyes the most, forcing me to keep them closed as I channeled. I found myself experiencing a strange combination of being tired, yet considerably energized after each channeling.

Mary loved to talk to the Masters, and it was so much easier for me getting the information during the day and sleeping through the night. The connection was more and more normal. We were also noticing that the promptings we were getting were becoming easier to notice. We were taking action on the promptings and our life was transforming.

Initially, I questioned if it was truly happening. Who was I to do this? Did I have an effect on the information coming through? Was it all real? I got beyond the doubts as time went on. It became obvious that it wasn't me creating this information that was coming in. I knew this because first, some of it I had never heard before, and second, I could not remember what had been said in the channelings. Mary had to tell me, or I listened to the recordings. If it was me and not the Masters, I would have remembered what was said because it would have been at the lower vibration—my normal one. In addition, the messages in these channelings were, in many cases, beyond my knowledge and understanding.

After several months of bringing the energies through for Mary to ask questions, she asked me if I would be willing to share this gift with someone else. A whole other set of fears and doubts came in. What if I interfered with their guidance? What if they judged me? What if they doubted or didn't like the message that came through? What if I could not channel the energies while in front of others?

It wasn't imposter syndrome; I knew this was real. It was the judgment I thought I might get, the rejections that might come. I was afraid I might lose credibility in other areas of my life around people's fear or criticisms about channeling. After all, just a few years prior, I would have judged and questioned the validity of channeling. It was about being rejected or degraded over something that people questioned or feared. My reputation and how people looked at me was more important than sharing this gift.

We all are limited from time to time by society's beliefs and judgments. It is difficult to be different and to go beyond the norm especially when we are called to things that are not widely accepted by the collective, but we all have gifts and talents to help us live on purpose. Not all these gifts and talents will be accepted or approved of by others leaving us forced to choose to follow our callings and trust our knowingness or stay stuck in the expectations and limitations currently surrounding us.

We can only hope that we are given the opportunity that gives us the courage to admit who we are and the tenacity to share it with the world. For me, the opportunity was provided in the pain of someone in our lives.

There was a young girl, a daughter of a friend, Sasha, visiting us. She was troubled and confused about what she wanted to do in and with her life. Mary believed that it would be very beneficial for her to have an opportunity to talk to the Masters. Immediately the voices of my sub-personalities were active in my head. I heard the same old fears from the same voices that were prevalent when Mary first suggested I try channeling. "She will judge you." "What if you can't do it?" and "What if she tells others?" were some of the things my sub-personalities repeated over and over. I had moved beyond the protection of these voices before, I could do it again.

And then there was the thing that I was most worried about. After I had been to Eloryia for my introduction to channeling, my curiosity grew. I sought out other opportunities to interact with the Masters through other channels. In these other channelings, I noticed where the channeler's beliefs, feelings, or opinions seemed to be interjected into the message. I never wanted that to happen in a channeling through me. I was afraid that I might change or taint the message. I never want to be responsible for anyone misunderstanding the message or using the guidance in the wrong way.

This fear was harder to move beyond than the voices in my head. I decided to use the techniques I learned in Dahn Yoga to go into a deep meditation to move beyond this fear. After I told Mary what I was about to do, I went to the bedroom of our small apartment and closed the door behind me. The apartment was situated so the afternoon sun shone through the bedroom window and warmed the corner of the room adjacent to our bed. I grabbed the magnets we used every day in our yoga meditations, sat on the floor, closed my eyes, and allowed myself to relax. It wasn't long before I saw the familiar shade of blue I recognized as Archangel Michael. As I acknowledged him, I felt myself release into the safety of the conversation.

"If I channel for any of my friends or family, I don't want to interfere in the guidance you provide," I stated without hesitation. I continued without waiting for acknowledgment or a reply, "If I do or if I feel I have interfered, I will never channel again."

I heard the strong and commanding voice of Michael in my head say, "You control when, where, and how you connect. The choice is yours." And in that moment, I began to feel confident that I wouldn't interfere. "You will also control who. We will never ask you to let us come through if you don't want to allow it."

But I wasn't completely sure, at least not yet. "What if I do interfere?" I continued to push.

"We will take you deeper, remove you from the conversation if it becomes a possibility." He responded. "And if you ever believe it happens, you can choose not to connect with us." This eased my fear entirely and I noticed my body relaxed.

I went into the meditation with the intention of alleviating the fear of possibly interfering in the guidance. But when that fear was gone, I began to notice more and more colors. I should have known

I was in for much more. Soon every color of the spectrum seemed to fill the room. I asked Michael, "What is happening, why all the colors?"

"The colors are different energies. Just like we shared the colors that represent the four guides in your channeling with Eloryia, every energy stream has a color," he explained. "If you practice and raise your vibration, you will be able to share all the streams of energy. This will allow the guides of anyone you choose to channel for to come through and clearly share their message."

This was the longest I had been able to connect through meditation and I was getting tired, but this was too important, and I couldn't stop. I had to know more. "I understand what you are saying, but how will I explain it to others?" I questioned.

"Because you have made the decision to share this gift with friends and family and in the future may choose to share with others," Michael began, "I will share how to describe us."

"First, as I just explained, if you practice, you will be able to channel all the energies, not just the ones of *your* guides. Each time you channel will be different. The guides of those that you are channeling for will be the energies that come through," he continued.

"Uh, huh," was all I could say.

"Each guide is a higher vibration of the energy stream of the recipient," he went on.

"Wait, are you saying that each of our guides are the same energy as we are?" I quizzed him.

Michael patiently continued, "Yes! Just a different vibration, a higher frequency. But the difference in vibration doesn't matter for the purposes of the channelings. We want you to know that we come through as equals to support you all on your journeys. Our purpose is to help you live your purpose for we all are one."

"What do you mean *we are all one*?" I immediately inquired.

"We, all of you, and us, are source energy. We are one. But that is for another time." He said before continuing. "A good analogy is from the days of King Arthur. Arthur met with his knights as equals, all coming together for one purpose. We want you and the people you channel for to envision sitting down with us, your guides, at a table coming together for one purpose. The purpose is to help each person fully live and experience their purpose on Earth."

"That is how to describe our channelings and that is what you can call us, *The Round Table*," he concluded.

Before I had a chance to formulate a question he said, "That is enough for today." And with those words the colors dissipated, and I felt the energy leave my body.

With my choice to channel for our family and friends and this guidance from Michael, The Round Table began.

I couldn't wait to share with Mary. There was so much to share. My fear was gone, and we both had a better understanding of how this gift of being able to channel was going to be our gift for others. I was able to share it all, everything Michael shared with me before I could no longer keep my eyes open, and I lay down for a nap.

Soon after, I met with Sasha. She was visiting because she was having a hard time at home and anxious about her future. When she had all her questions about channeling and what she should expect answered, I sat on the floor, closed my eyes, and went through my process to connect. I noticed the energy in my body increasing as I started to cough. There were new colors in my head, different than ever before. When I felt comfortable with the energy, I heard the words in my head, "Good Afternoon."

The first channeling for someone other than Mary had started.

What Archangel Michael promised had happened in this first channeling of many. They discussed with Sasha in great detail her reason for being on Earth, what she had forgotten, how to remember that, and how to uncover her purpose and mission. I didn't know it at the time, but Imagine Miracles was birthed that very afternoon. I started to see how my own Unique Purpose was coming together to be of service to humanity. I had the vision and was ready to get started. Mary and I had a lot of work ahead of us, and I was excited!

Chapter Twenty-Three
Putting It All Together

When you open your self to all the possibilities
and align with the real you, the Universe
constantly conspires to help you create and
manifest.

The Round Table, channeled by Vince Kramer

We all have a calling to live what we know is our purpose on Earth. Even when we aren't sure what it is or maybe don't understand it fully, we are being called to it. We actually have an ache because it is missing, or we aren't living it fully. It isn't that we don't *know* our purpose, we just forgot it. Our awakening is the journey to remember it, to remember who we are, what we have to offer, and why we are here. It is essential to know all three parts, but we don't need to know or understand them before we expand and begin to live that purpose. In fact, people have been living it all along. It isn't about *finding* their purpose, it is about remembering it and seeing how their entire life has been created and co-created by them and those around them to help each person live it. It is time for all of us to remember, but first we must learn how to remember and connect to guidance.

We are unique and special. There is no one in this world exactly like us. When we accept our unique combination of gifts and talents and move deeper into purpose, we expand even more and the Universe and everything around us conspires to help. The secret is awareness. When we are aware in every moment, we will begin to see how we are supported in discovering, creating, and living the life we are meant to live.

Mary and I were both on a journey. We weren't quite sure what the journey was or where it would take us. It was also obvious that while we each had our own journey, we also had one together.

It was our journey together that created an undeniable energy and connection that we both recognized in our hearts. This heart energy was the glue that would keep us moving forward no matter the obstacles put before us—or were we creating those too? We embarked on this energetic and physical journey together bringing along our lives and the complications of our lives onto this path.

It became very clear to us that the path I was on was similar to the path found described in most metaphysical teachings that we all need to take when we are trying to discover, create, and live a life of purpose. But with the downloads from The Round Table, Mary and I realized that we would be sharing this path in ways that would allow others to access, in one place, all the pieces that I had searched for during my own journey. We knew that there needed to be understanding of energy by combining spirituality and science. We knew the importance of each person living their purpose fully. Imagine Miracles was born.

We trusted that the guidance through channeling the Masters and following the promptings that were given to us would help us to understand. We continued to connect through channelings, both for Mary and others. I routinely had my deep connections through meditation. And from time to time, there would be a nighttime download.

We asked for messages, signs, and help to accelerate us on this path that we knew we were meant to be on. The phrase, *Be careful what you ask for*, couldn't have been more appropriate. It wasn't long before we attracted acceleration into our lives, but it wasn't necessarily in the way we thought it would come.

When Mary and I first dated, she talked about owning a place where people could come together in community and freely express their spirituality. In fact, just before I came into her life, she was working on building that community and physical space. Our budding relationship, our new love, derailed her plans. When we married, we had a pretty good picture about how our lives and our desires could be intertwined. I wanted to teach programs, hold workshops, speak, and coach. Mary still held the dream of community and bringing people together in a safe space where they could be themselves. The logical choice was a retreat center. We started our search for a location to meet our needs. It not only placed us directly on our mutual path, but actually turned out to be our greatest teacher.

With Mary's real estate skills and my love of research, it wasn't long before we had many possibilities. We settled on four to consider more extensively.

The first was a coffee plantation in Costa Rica. The second was a similar property located in the hill country of Texas. The third property was an organic farm in Oregon, and the fourth was a retreat center owned by a church in southwest Colorado. Although we called Colorado home, we were living in Southern California at the time. We decided to drive the fourteen hours to visit the thirty acres with a majestic 8,000 square-foot log lodge and two other buildings with a total of twenty-one bedrooms.

We hopped into our Mercedes ML in the afternoon of that clear August day and were on our way. With the plans to drive straight through we scheduled shifts when each would drive while the other slept. We were excited about the possibility of this place being the one but tried to be reserved because of the disappointment in the other properties. The drive across southern California, northern Arizona, and southern Utah was beautiful. At least what we saw of it during daylight hours. As we passed the sign pointing to the only location in the United States that four states come together at one point, the excitement started to build. Only fifty-five miles and we would know if we found our center or not.

Our conversation turned to our love of Colorado and the beauty of the southwest corner of the state. The high desert was magnificent at this time of the morning and in the distant east were the silhouettes of the majestic San Juan Mountains. The colors were just like an artist's palette. We thought we might even be seeing a bit of white at the very top of one of the peaks. We had driven this route many times on our houseboat vacation trips to Lake Powell, but it was somehow different today.

Mary had been talking to the realtor for several weeks and the plan was to meet at the property. She had warned us that the GPS on our phone would give us confusing information and we would get lost. Mary had the directions in her hands and pointed out every turn. It wasn't long before we were pulling into the drive to what would become our new retreat center. We both individually knew it as soon as we turned into the drive and saw the lodge. We didn't share that knowing until the drive back to California.

The quarter-mile driveway led to a roundabout bordered by the striking log lodge and another building called the Guest House. The roundabout center had a fountain, flowers, and trees. There in the doorway of the lodge was our realtor.

After a two-hour tour, we were back on the road to California. The center was perfect for what we had as a vision going forward. There were twenty-one bedrooms, three big meeting rooms (one in each building), and a commercial kitchen big enough to feed a large group of people. And it came fully furnished. There were a few drawbacks that came up during our fourteen-hour drive home. The distance to a major airport was a big one. Another was the deferred maintenance on the buildings. Although it wasn't as bad as the one we'd seen in Oregon, there was work to be done. The third was the sheer size of the property as a whole.

The drive home went much faster. The conversation kept us busy and there was very little sleep. We talked about the pros. We talked about the cons. We imagined the possibilities. By the time we arrived at our condo in Torrance, California, we had decided Dolores, Colorado and the Sophia Retreat Center would be our new home.

We thought we purchased Sophia because it was something we should do for the business. What we learned, and it was confirmed many times in the five and a half years that we owned it, is that we needed this location to learn some very important things about ourselves and the high vibration of the property would support us through the lessons.

The first six months at the center kept us extremely busy. I was flying full time out of the United Airlines pilot base in Houston. I was flying four four-day trips a month. A seven-hour commute on each end of every trip left little time at the center. Every waking hour there was dedicated to the deferred items we discovered on our tour. We were blessed that Mary's oldest Lloyd had decided to join us in our venture.

With all this work, I had little time for meditations or channelings. I was tired when I got home from my trips and that was before doing anything at Sophia. We were all working hard towards the dream.

There was a labyrinth on the property. It was specifically built across the bridge from a gazebo behind two of the main buildings and adjacent to the third. It seemed like an unusual place, but we soon discovered it was on an energy vortex. It was a vortex just like the ones that are found in the Sedona, Arizona area. It was a feminine energy that was very powerful. It became a way for us to recharge after working so hard.

One of the advantages in traveling to fly, I had a lot of time to myself on layovers. I spent as much of it as I could meditating to get the most information and guidance possible. I wanted to live my purpose even though I wasn't completely sure what it was yet. I meditated on different topics I knew should be in our programs. When I downloaded what I was asking for, I implemented them in my life and then put the processes together so others could implement them. I got so much information that I'd never heard before and had new understandings that had previously eluded me. On my commutes home which consisted of a two-hour flight to Denver from Houston, a one-hour layover minimum, an hour flight to Durango, and then an hour drive home, I cataloged all the information in my mind and mapped out how I could share it all with Mary.

As soon as I got home, I would jump out of my trusty steed, a white Ford 250 Super Duty, and run into the lodge, hollering for Mary all the way. We would meet in the master bedroom, and right after a hello kiss, I would spend at least an hour sharing everything I'd learned and what I'd done with the information.

We made it a point to channel at least once every time I made it home. We would go into the lodge's master bedroom. It was a huge room with an open bathroom. The handmade log bed was against the south wall of the bedroom which left a large open space in the center of the room. Mary would place chairs in a circle and she, her son Lloyd, and I would sit together. For one to two hours, I would channel, and they would ask questions. These sessions helped me get more comfortable bringing the energy in and my body began to handle the higher frequencies better. In these sessions, Lloyd was introduced to channeling and the guidance that came in from them. Mary would ask questions to help us understand the information I downloaded and how to best use it. She would get clarity on happenings at Sophia and how we could best move forward with our growth and in creating Imagine Miracles.

One of the realizations in the first year was that Sophia was the feminine energy that the little blonde girl represented since it was evident that Mary and I weren't going to physically have a child. The energy of that child was represented by Sophia and the lessons it provided. Not having a child was a major disappointment, but knowing the lessons were leading us to purpose was reassuring.

The next several years were like our higher education in bringing science and spirituality together to help us live in the ways we were meant to live them. The experiences that we attracted and created, along with the guidance we were connecting with, opened the doors to more of the unlimited possibilities available to us. Each trip away and each time we were together provided opportunities for us to learn more and grow into our true selves. At the same time, we were creating the structure of our company and formulating the programs to assist others on their journeys of self-discovery and empowerment.

For me there were the normal life stressors of working a full-time job and owning a separate business, but I loved my personal path and my personal transformation. It was a high-flying time for me. For Mary, it was not the same. She was experiencing for the first time in her life the high vibration of the land and she was being introduced to living "what could be" with the blending of Divine Feminine and Masculine as she lived primarily at Sophia.

I began to realize that she didn't have the on-demand connection with Source that was becoming normal for me, and she didn't have the tools to transform her old way of being into the new way of being that the energetics of the Center were giving her. I was moving into the understanding of the new paradigm and was leaving her behind.

During one of the longer stretches of time where we were separate for several weeks, I received an illuminating email from her. Sometimes emails were the only way we could stay deeply connected beyond our quick goodnight calls. I was sitting at a gate between flights and was delighted to see there was an email waiting for me from Mary, but the subject line caught my attention and caused my heart to sense danger. The subject line read, "The Definition of Insanity." I anxiously but quickly opened the email to be able to read what she was telling me. Mary has been conditioned in her life to be very direct and unemotional. Even though the email describing her frustrations with running the center were clear and concise, I could tell she was in a low vibration. She was discovering that she was repeating all the old thinking and behaviors that she had relied on for her fifty years. This energetic place was helping her to quickly become aware that she couldn't be the same old person and respond in the same old ways.

I did the best I could to be supportive. With the limited free time I had I knew the best way to support her was to give her as much time as possible with The Round Table. They could reach her heart and support her mind faster than I could. This was very hard for me because I wanted to be everything for her, but I knew her path would be accelerated by having as much time as possible with high vibrational guidance through channeling with the Masters.

Over the years, one of the most important things I learned was that we have to get our individual answers and not live by anyone else's. We all have the ability to connect and get our answers. I chose to use our unfortunate separation to dedicate myself to learning how to fully get my answers and implement the new knowing in my life. I also chose to put all I learned together in a way that everyone could find their answers and design and create a life based on them.

Each trip I uncovered another aspect and gained a new understanding.

On one layover, I woke up from a dream about purpose. Without opening my eyes, I asked for more information. I heard a familiar voice in my head. The voice of Michael shared concepts that I hadn't heard before.

"There are three parts to your purpose," I heard him say. "You think your purpose is the reason you are on Earth. You think it is your mission, but it is much more. You must know all parts to know your purpose and to begin to live it fully."

"What are the three parts?" I asked without saying a word.

"Soon you will meet someone who teaches about the different parts, and you will understand," he answered immediately. The conversation continued until I had a game plan on finding what I needed to know and the best way to uncover my unique purpose and then to help others find theirs.

In less than a month I was introduced to this man. With his help and The Round Table, I uncovered the three parts of my purpose in opening hearts and raising the vibration of the world. I began to explore and develop ways to help unmask the three parts of a person's purpose. Soon I had five ways to assist everyone to finally know their reason for being and a formula to get the answers that are most important. All of them are used in one form or the other for connecting to different parts of the self. They were developed and used by many well-known psychologists.

Another instance when I was home alone, I decided to ask a question in a meditation. I used a technique I learned to quiet my mind and move into a theta brainwave state. Theta brainwaves occur when we are sleeping or dreaming, but they don't occur during the deepest phases of sleep. And then I asked, "Why is it important to know our purpose?"

Lying there with my eyes closed, my vision filled with the brightest, most brilliant magenta light. It was a color I had never experienced before. And then I heard, "You are all here for a specific reason and you must live your reason so others can learn theirs."

"What does that mean?" I asked.

"It means if you live your purpose, it will help or allow others to live their purpose. Look at your Earth as a big puzzle. Each of you are puzzle pieces. When you live your purpose, your reason for being, you put your piece in the puzzle. Now that your piece is in the puzzle two, three, or even more can see how their piece fits," the voice explained.

"I understand the analogy. You said 'reason for being,' what do you mean by that?" I asked wanting to understand and know more.

Without any hesitation, the voice explained, "First you are all here to experience an energy stream. An energy stream of the one energy that some call the Universe, others Source, and still others God. You came to expand that energy stream."

He went on to explain that we chose to come to Earth, and we chose a specific purpose to help ourselves and others in this expansion.

He stated in all certainty, "You chose when to be born, where you were born, and even chose your parents. You made all these choices to help you live the life that would give you everything to live that purpose."

"I understand what you are saying," I was quick to declare. "But I'm not sure I can grasp it and it challenges what I believe."

"You are not alone. Most of you will find it difficult to believe," the voice assured. "Over time we will share more to help you understand and change your belief. Then, you can help others."

I had many doubts at that moment, but I did get enough information to help me understand the significance of what I just learned.

I didn't know it, but I learned the reason I chose to come to Earth during this interaction. I didn't know the exact words and couldn't explain it, but I felt it and it felt good. I came to help others understand what was just shared with me and help them find and live that purpose.

These are just two examples of my experiences with guidance during this time. Over the years there have been many with each leading me to learn, discover, and grow. I learned more about quantum physics and energy, the brain and psychology, the universal laws and how they affect us. I learned about our beliefs and egos. As I said before, every time I learned something new, the perfect book, teacher, or opportunity would show up in my life to help me take my understanding to a new level and to see that all the guidance I received was backed by science. All to help me understand and live my unique purpose.

I believe it is important for anyone who has transformational or personal growth information to share with others that they do their own work first.

At about the four-year point of owning Sophia, I finally felt that I had done enough of my work to begin to share it with others. I had personally implemented everything I had learned from the voices at night, my meditations, and the channelings from The Round Table. I used all the techniques I had learned and all the knowledge I gained from research and mentors to prepare to fully live the life I am meant to live. It was an eight-year journey. I put everything I learned and everything I developed together in one place so it wouldn't take anyone else eight years.

The formulas and the blueprints were developed. The exercises designed and the information compiled; the scripts were written, and modalities chosen. We created practical teachings from the divine knowledge. It was time to launch Imagine Miracles and share it all with people; those ready to awaken to purpose and the life that they are meant to live.

I remembered the guidance. "Surround yourself with a community of people whose gifts and talents will help you share your gifts and talents."

The familiar saying "When the student is ready the teacher appears" was true for us, but in our case, it was the mentors and coaches. When it was time for a coaching certificate it was John Maxwell. When it was time for a business structure and being able to share what we had to offer in a way that others could understand, it was Lisa Sasevich. When we wanted to get the word out, it was Jeff Walker. And when it was time to make Imagine Miracles our business, Mary and I sharing our gifts and talents together, it was Andrea J. Lee.

The community didn't stop there. It was finding like-minded and like-hearted people who were growing and expanding themselves. It was helping and supporting them as they helped and supported us. It was having others to understand and help without trying to fix. It was making a difference together as we each made a difference our own way.

The Round Table shares that the Universe is constantly conspiring to help us and create the life that we are meant to live. We just have to be open to seeing the signs and the promptings. We each are unique and special, and it is important that we learn to realize that we are and share it with the world.

Moment of Reflection

There truly are no mistakes or coincidences in the Universe, in our lives. Everything brings a gift. It might be helping people see that they are stronger than they might have thought. It might help individuals develop a gift or discover a talent that can transform their life or the lives around them. Many times, we can't see the magic in the circumstance or experience at the time. We can only see it as tragic. But we will find the gift if we are ready to look.

The experience that Mary and I had in the five years at Sophia was far from optimal, but it provided many gifts. One of the biggest for both of us was that it gave us the opportunity to get to know ourselves. We learned our fears, what was holding us back, and where we were stuck. We learned what we were capable of and developed more gifts to help us live our purpose and the purpose we have together. It gave me time to learn more and develop programs and courses to share what we learned through our journeys and guidance from The Round Table.

The Universe is still conspiring to help us, as we create and co-create experiences that are no mistakes or coincidences.

Chapter Twenty-Four

A Mentor's Challenge

The most amazing thing you can be is you.
There is no one like you and there is no one that
can do what you can do. There will be many
people in your life that will help you bring the
real you to the world.

The Round Table, channeled by Vince Kramer

O ver the years, I have taken the information I received from
The Round Table channelings and combined it with research
and training from some of the most forward-thinking mentors I
could find. One thing I know without doubt, we all chose to come
to this planet to make a difference. We brought that mission with
us at birth. We call it our Divine Intent. It is what many call our
why or our purpose. When we are bringing our Divine Intent to the
world and making a difference, we are living the life we are meant
to live—the one we chose.

Each of us develops a personality which is our 3D operating system.
Everything that we have experienced has led to us developing a
unique combination of gifts and talents. We created our very own

process to deliver these gifts and talents to accomplish making the difference we are meant to make.

To make that difference at the magnitude we are capable of, we must bring all we have to offer to the game. We must show up authentically and truly be all that we can be. Quantum physics shares that there are no mistakes or coincidences.

The good thing is that we weren't made to do it alone. Humans are community animals. We are meant to work together. When we surround ourselves with like-minded and like-hearted people, we get the support we need. We each have someone that understands our journey is unique to us. They are there to help us find our way. They don't force us into *their* way.

I believe that part of that community should include mentors and coaches. But not just any mentor or coach, ones that understand our uniqueness, our Divine Intent, and that we have the answers to discovering, creating, and living the life we are meant to live. Mary and I have been blessed with several.

We invested in ourselves and had two of the best business coaches in the entrepreneurial world. It is important to surround ourselves with people that can support us in being all that we are meant to be. I believe that, and I have done everything to ensure that our business Imagine Miracles will thrive for years to come.

Mary and I were sitting with three other heart-based entrepreneurs on day one of a three-day retreat at the Marriott Hotel in downtown Dallas. We were in a breakout group with our mentor Andrea J. Lee from a year-long mastermind we had chosen to help us bring our work to the world in a way that serves the largest number of people in living the life they are meant to live.

As I looked around the intimate suite which was well beyond the comfort level of our room, I was impressed by the similarity of the three businesses represented by the people in the room, and, at the same time, how different they each were. The dim light of the room gave us an opportunity to be introspective as Andrea challenged us with some tough questions about our businesses and where we wanted them to go. The seven of us had been together for about six months and were willing to share at a very deep level.

We had just gone through an extensive mind searching exercise on what type of sales we would need to make to meet our business goals. There were many intertwined aspects that had to be brought together in the discovery process. The overall goal was to look at the combination of sales for each program we offered and at what price points. As each of us went to the flipchart, we were supported through the process by our very capable coach and others in the room that cared as much about our business as they did about their own. It was an excellent activity to bring clarification and Mary whispered to me how glad she was that we were with this group at this time in our business creation.

As we completed the challenge of looking at necessary revenue, I was expecting a break. I was packing up my journal and binder when Andrea leaned forward in her chair and looked at Samm and Mary, a mother and daughter team, and asked them how they were going to show up in full authenticity in their business.

She addressed each of them separately. Both were quiet. They slid back deep in the contemporary couch they were sitting on. I wasn't sure if they were trying to hide, brace themselves for the tough question, or get as far away from Andrea as they could. She followed up with questions like, "When and where aren't you being authentic?" and "How would your business change if you would be 100 percent authentic?"

I'll admit I didn't hear a word that either of them said as they answered her questions. I was desperately searching for *my* answers to those difficult exploring questions. In my mind I was justifying that I was giving the business everything I had to give. I was sure I had put it all out there. But I caught myself squirming in my high-back chair.

Just minutes before, I noticed how comfortable it was. That wasn't the case any longer and it had nothing to do with the chair. I knew she had something in mind for all of us. I just wasn't sure if it was going to be the same for all of us. What was she thinking for me? I love to participate in these discussions, but I felt ill-prepared, and I just wanted to hide. Of course, it was impossible for me to hide this 6'5" 240-pound body no matter how big the chair was.

Through the confusion of all the voices in my head, I heard her ask Mary where she wasn't showing up fully. I realized I was next, and she was asking everyone relatively the same questions. I felt some relief around the perceived certainty. And then, it popped in my head almost magically. I had been hiding my channeling from the world. I mostly channeled for Mary, and there were a few times that I had channeled for family and a couple of friends.

Although I had learned to accept the fact that I could bring this information and guidance through quite easily, I still had reluctance and judgment around sharing it with others. I believed I wouldn't be taken seriously by some and would be overlooked or dismissed by others.

As I prepared to answer the questions I knew would come my way shortly, it was a strange realization that I felt this way so emphatically. I knew from my past—the times before my experiences of the last several years—I wouldn't have taken channeling seriously.

There were other concerns echoing in my head. It was my dream to teach and speak, I wanted to share this little-known information that could and will transform lives. I didn't want to be seen as a channel—*just a channel*—and ignored for the gifts and talents that I have to bring to the world.

I must have been buried deep in my thoughts for at least a half hour when I heard "Vince, *Vince.*"

I looked up to see everyone staring at me intently. All with quizzical looks on their faces. Mary had her hand on my leg, obviously trying to get my attention that way. Andrea smiled knowingly and asked, "So Vince, where aren't you showing up authentically in your business?"

My throat was dry, and the words seemed to be jumbled in my head. These were strange reactions. I'm usually ready to share without reservation. I didn't realize I was this adamant about keeping the channeling quiet—at least not bringing it into the business. There were people in the room that still didn't know that I could channel. I wasn't sure I even wanted to share the fact I did with them, let alone the world.

Even though I understood what she meant about sharing all of ourselves, it was difficult. I know being authentic and sharing all of us is what will set us apart from others who offer things similar to what we offer. I closed my eyes, gathered my composure, and leaned forward in my chair. I opened my eyes, I looked right in Andrea's eyes.

"Where am I not being authentic? Where am I not showing up authentically?" I repeated back. "I am a channel, and I am very hesitant to share that with anyone."

I had everyone's attention, and I continued listing all the reasons that had come up over the years. And then, I did something I never expected to do, I offered to channel for the group. Right then and there. Everyone was nodding their heads yes and Andrea agreed immediately.

"Great, let's set up some time." I said relieved that I was open about my unusual gift, and it was readily accepted.

"No, I mean right now," Andrea exclaims without leaving me a choice. I admired her for making sure that I stepped out fully and would no longer hold back any of my gifts or talents.

As I looked around the room I started to emotionally and physically prepare myself for my first public channeling. Yes, it was a group of people I had known for a while, but I never considered channeling for them, especially in this context. And it was going to happen right then.

Immediately Andrea asked everyone to take a quick break and then to find a comfortable seat. When everyone returned, I moved the oversized stuffed chair that Andrea had been sitting in to a place where everyone could see it easily. I sat down in the chair and prepared myself to move into a state where I was out of the way and could allow the Masters and Angels to come in.

As I prepared, Mary shared important information about The Round Table and what to expect with the group who were bubbling over with anticipation.

Mary shared excitedly, "The group Vince channels call themselves The Round Table. When they first shared the name with him, they said it was because they would be there to support anyone who wanted it. The Round Table's name came from a reference to King Arthur's Round Table and the equality of the knights that sat around it. Like the knights, the Masters want everyone to know that they sit at the table as equals to those who want to receive their guidance through the channelings. The one thing about The Round Table as they come through Vince is, they don't hold back and they share it, just the way it is."

As I heard Mary helping the people in the room understand what they would experience, doubt knocked on the door trying to get in my head. I began to worry how the directness would affect the people that were about to participate in the channelings. I concentrated on the techniques I had learned to make the connections necessary for the high vibrational energies to come through me.

This was the first real test with people who don't know the Masters as they share through me and for some who had never experienced a channeling.

Mary continued to educate and put them at ease, "The Masters and Archangels that come through Vince are at a very high frequency. He will keep his eyes closed when he is channeling because the energy is too much for them." She got a big smile on her face and then told them more. "When the Masters start sharing, they normally share a message and then ask if there are any questions. Don't hesitate to ask questions; that is when you will get the most specific information. Talk to them just like they are your best friends because they are. Keep in mind they won't tell you anything that might affect your free will." After letting everyone digest what she shared she asked, "Does anyone have any questions?"

Just as Mary asked if there were any questions, I felt myself move into a deep meditative state followed shortly thereafter by a rush of energy that warmed my whole body. The feeling was of being loved in a way I had never been loved before. And like every channeling I had done before, I heard words in my head just before they came out of my mouth.

"Good afternoon, it is an honor and a privilege to be here at the table with you today!"

Just like that, the channeling began.

Like my very first channeling for Mary, I remembered very little at the end of the Masters' time with the group. As I came back into my body, Mary asked them to share their experience. Everyone was extremely happy and complimentary of the love and the guidance they received. I was happy no one was offended or upset. I was even more happy that it seemed like everything was going to be okay. I could share The Round Table with others.

When I listened to the channeling recording later, they didn't disappoint and presented everything for this small group. They spent time with every person giving them guidance on their lives and businesses. They were direct and to the point. They shared what each person needed in the moment to fully step into who they are in every area of life.

I continued the weekend workshop feeling free and liberated. I even had an opportunity with the one hundred plus people in the group to share the fact I channel. It was well-received, and I haven't hesitated to share since.

I understand why I chose to limit my channeling before. By playing it safe and not channeling for people outside our closest circle I had time to feel comfortable with bringing the energies in more readily. It helped me gain confidence that I could bring their messages in clearly and, most importantly to me, the messages weren't influenced by me in any way. It gave me time to learn more about myself and find strength in who I am and why I was given this gift.

Moment of Reflection

To fully show up in the world, we must know three things. We have to know who we are, what we have to offer, and why we are here. We call that *Your Unique Purpose*. Once we know those three things, we are in touch with why we came to Earth. We can trust ourselves and know that we have our answers. When we learn to trust ourselves and our guidance, others will trust us. We will also trust them.

Everyone needs someone to see what they aren't seeing in and for themselves. This person or persons can be a mentor, guide, parent, or friend. Someone that can share their combination of gifts and talents in a way that allows us to better share ours. They may teach, coach, or just be the example for us to become more aware. They see us for who we are and help us bring all of it to the world in a completely authentic way. They help us see what's missing.

We sometimes get too close to a problem, and we can't see the next step, or the voices in our heads convince us that we can't or shouldn't take that step. Maybe, we just want to give up. This is when we need the support.

That is why we attract the support and guidance into our lives: to help us see more clearly. When we feel that we have to show up the way we are expected to by other people, "our people" can point out who we truly are.

We truly aren't meant to do it alone.

You are special and unique. We all are special and unique. We are all needed to put the big puzzle of life together. We need each other to be able to uncover and move into our unique space.

Epilogue

The guidance has continued to come over the years. It shows up in channelings, late-night visits, the perfect book, or a poignant podcast at the perfect time, and mentors showing up when these students are ready. The Moments of Choice continue to come. They show up in messages, promptings, and wake-up calls. We all have this guidance available to us. This type of connection is normal. You just have to find your way to get it. We all have our specific ways, and it is where we feel we can trust and surrender. We have learned many different ways and have helped others tap into their guidance easily.

As the information is shared by the Masters, Mary and I implement it into our lives. It has been a journey of learning and growing and then taking what we've experienced and putting it together in a way to serve you. Our journey has taken many years and our hope is that yours doesn't take as long. The choice is yours.

We learned what we wanted in life and if it was in alignment with who we are. We learned what had been getting in our way. And we learned how to navigate the obstacles. Most importantly, we learned how to share it with others in the way they need to hear, see, and experience it.

We have grown as individuals and as a couple. As we each learned more about ourselves and uncovered our individual purposes, we learned it was truly no mistake or coincidence that we were together. We also have our purpose together: to share this work with anyone who is ready to live the life they are meant to live. There is a reason why you have attracted the people who are in your life, and we are here to help you understand that.

As the years have passed, I have channeled more and more for others. With each channeling, the message, although the same, was tailored specifically for each individual or group. It has always come in a way that the people could hear and accept at their current consciousness, delivered in a way that they could understand. I learned from them, not just the material, but the way the Masters delivered it and how it was tailored to each person as they asked questions. It is so important to share their message that we offer a free channeling to the public every month.

I gained a new understanding and appreciation of purpose, creating, why we are on Earth, and the importance of understanding that there is no separation. I learned that there are three parts to our purpose: the who, the what, and the why of you, or as we have come to call them, Quintessence, Gift, and Divine Intent.

I used my gifts and talents to create the Miracle Life Method to share everything I have learned from The Round Table and what I have learned as a result of the channelings I have shared with others. The method delivers how each of us in our own way can discover, create, and live the life we are meant to live. It consists of the Your Unique Purpose Formula, C.R.E.A.T.E. Model, and Quantum Thought. All three bring science and spirituality together for true and lasting breakthroughs in living your life on purpose. This was how Mary and I were meant to live our unique purposes.

We cofounded Imagine Miracles to bring this new paradigm of thinking to the world. We developed and brought together ways that you can learn to tap into your guidance with certainty and confidence. We have also developed and brought together everything you need to discover, create, and live the life you are meant to live your way. We believe that to make the huge difference you are meant to make in this world, you must transform and live Your Life Your Way.

We want to share with you in many ways. This book is one of many to come. In fact, we are also launching a series of books that bring the messages of The Round Table in an entertaining and enjoyable way. We want to take The Round Table out into the world, so you can interact with the energy in person. It is an experience everyone should have at least once. The energy of love they bring is transformational.

We know that as each of us uncover the reason we chose to come to Earth, share our gift with the world, and live our divine intent fully, we all will create the change we want to see in the world.

You are meant to live Your Unique Purpose fully in a community that supports your journey as you support them. And we are excited to be on this journey with you.

With Love,

Vince and Mary

For more information about us and Imagine Miracles,
visit imaginemiracles.com

A Free Gift from Vince and Mary

Take the Next Step Towards Your Miracle Life Guide
Get to Know Yourself and Discover the Life You're Meant to Live

Discover exactly where you are on your journey towards your miracle life and become empowered to take matters into your own hands. Are you living the life you're meant to live? The questions are all the same, but the answers are only yours. You're here for a reason, and you are in control of your next steps. You're in the right place. Download our free guide to Take the Next Step Towards Your Miracle Life.

Download this free guide and receive…
- A clear understanding of where you are on your journey towards your Miracle Life
- A chance to get to know yourself better
- An opportunity to see what's possible for you
- A deep dive into the who, what, why, where, and how of your purpose
- A clear understanding of the journey ahead towards your Miracle Life
- The exact information you need to take the next step forward

Follow this link to download your free guide: https://miraclelifemethod.com/take-the-next-step-towards-your-miracle-life/

Learn more about channeling and the messages available from The Round Table

Our free monthly channelings consist of an educational presentation by The Round Table, a group of supportive and familiar energies such as the archangels, ascended masters, your guides and uniquely your higher self. Their goal is to assist you in finding your way, understand why you chose to come to Earth, and the meaning in all of it. After the educational presentation, there are opportunities for members of the audience to ask questions and receive guidance on their individual situation and circumstances through lasered one-on-one conversation and coaching. Personal and Group channelings are available and the messages from The Round Table are available in audio recordings.

Join us the Third Monday of every month and meet The Round Table. Save your seat at https://qr1.be/N6A8 or follow this QR Code.

Mary Kramer

Author/ Mentor/ Thought Leader/ Self-Reflection Guide

Mary's journey into her role as a highly sought-after Self-Reflection Guide began with an eye-opening visit to her cardiologist. It was revealed to Mary that the picture-perfect life in which she thought she was thriving in was actually the reason for her stress and worsening heart condition. This is where she experienced a moment of choice in which she opted to change her life in order to survive.

These changes led her on a spiritual journey where she learned to access her own modalities and vibrations, resulting in unlocking the life she was meant to live as an individual as well as the life she was meant to share with her husband, Vince, serving others to achieve a life of passion and purpose.

Mary shares her life experience in her teachings as a way to inspire people to get to know themselves and live an empowered life of their design. Having been recognized for her intuitive connection to people's hearts, Mary shines as a guide that aids her students in exploring their inner makeup to reframe their thoughts and circumstantial perceptions so they can vibrate at a higher level to experience divine connection and joy in their lives.

Vince Kramer

Transformational Growth and Human Potential Speaker/ Best-selling Author/
Mentor/ Teacher/ Coach/ Podcaster

From Airline Pilot, Military Veteran, Corporate Exec and Entrepreneur to a transformational teacher/guide and clear conscious channel, Vince Kramer brings a unique experience to the world of self-improvement and purpose-driven growth by combining science and spirituality. His past experience in stereotypically regimented fields brings a more integrated perspective to the Inward aspects of personal growth not often seen.

As a speaker, teacher, coach, clear conscious channel, and best-selling author of *Mastering the Art of Success* with Jack Canfield, Vince's distinct combination of experience, education and research helps him develop powerful talks, workshops and online training in finding success and fulfillment by living life by their design.

Vince passionately believes everyone is unique and the creator of their own life and success. It is his desire to inspire and empower men, women, organizations, businesses, and families to find success and happiness by designing and creating a life fueled by their desires.

Vince has over 35 years of experience training and coaching people in leadership, personal growth and transformation. He co-founded Imagine Miracles with his wife and business partner Mary, to educate and train leaders and people of all walks of life how to discover, design, create, and live their miracle in every aspect of their lives and businesses. Vince wrote and produced the Miracle Life Series of online training programs and associated workshops based on the C.R.E.A.T.E. Model and the Your Unique Purpose Formula.

For more great books from Empower Press
Visit Books.GracePointPublishing.com

If you enjoyed reading *Awakening Through Moments of Choice,* and
purchased it through an online retailer, please return to the site and write a
review to help others find the book.

Made in the USA
Monee, IL
12 November 2022

17611401R00154